ALSO BY CHRISTOPHER HARLAN

From Christopher Harlan, the #1 Amazon bestseller in multiple categories, *Away From Here: A Young Adult Novel*—A semi-autobiographical novel of first loves, losses, and growing up in the shadows of mental illness.

When I was seventeen years old there were only three things that I knew for certain: I was a mixed up mixed kid, with weird hair and an unhealthy love of comics; I wanted to forget I'd ever heard the words depression and anxiety; and I was hopelessly in love with a girl named Annalise who was, in every way that you can be, a goddess. What can I say about Anna? She wasn't the prom queen or the perfect girl from the movies, she was my weird, funny, messed up goddess. The girl of my dreams. The reason I'm writing these words.

I'd loved Anna from a distance my junior year, afraid to actually talk to her, but then one day during lunch my best friend threw a french fry at my face and changed everything. The rest, as they say, is history. Our History. Our Story. Annalise helped make me the man I am today, and loving her saved my teenaged soul from drowning in the depths of a terrible Bleh, the worst kind of sadness that there is, a concept Anna taught me about a long time ago, when we were younger than young. So flip the book over, open up the cover and let me tell you Our Story, which is like Annalise, herself - complicated, beautiful, funny, and guaranteed to teach you something by the time you're through. Maybe it'll teach you the complexity of the word potato, something I never understood until the very last page.

PRAISE FOR AWAY FROM HERE: A YOUNG ADULT NOVEL

"This is a book that could possibly replace Catcher in the Rye for today's kids, and it would be a darn sight more relevant to them."

—Jilly of the Valley

"What can I say about "Away From Here?" It is personal, emotional, refreshing, and made me reflect upon the journey we all take through life. . .Christopher Harlan is truly a gifted and passionate writer and I know this book will be in my heart forever."

—Lisa

"My first YA novel with this author and it's my favorite of all his books. So well written. It hit on some serious topics and reminds us of our youth and those struggles. But also how special that time was and it leaves its mark."

—KeriLovesBooks, Amazon Top 500 Reviewer

"Christopher has infused this "genreless" novel with plenty of humor. We all can relate to some character in Away From

Here, a poignant, bittersweet reminiscence of a truly awakening year in life, any one of our lives. He perfectly captures the emotional intensity of first love and blends those feelings with the crush of trying to figure out what is going to happen when you graduate from the relative safety of high school. I loved this book!! And you will too."

—Ingrid Duebbert

"Away From Here is an engaging read that will make you think. Makes you feel. Full of young love, teenage angst and everything you could possibly think of when it comes to high school."

—Becky Wise, Amazon Top 1000 Reviewer

"You can feel the emotions radiating from this book, it's as if Christopher Harlan dove into the minds of the Youth both current and past. Dealing with mental illness is still a hush hush topic all over the world, when we should be speaking up to help those affected by it learn to live life . The story of Annalise and Logan hits deep in the soul, and I believe there story Will hit home and help many of our youth today overcome their struggles."

—Leialoha Dacus

"This book was so well written and so heartfelt I couldn't put it down. I cannot wait to read another by this author."

—Eric Thornton

"Almost everything young adult novel I've ever read has made me ridiculously sad, but this one gave me hope. Very well written. I really enjoyed reading this. Thank you for a very insightful read, Christopher Harlan. I hope to read more works by you."

—Lisa Jacobus

"A great story. Characters are written so well, they seem like they are your friends. The emotions are written so well, made me smile and cry, depending on what was going on. I know this was written from the heart by the author. Loved it! Would definitely recommend it to anyone, you will identify with some part of the story."

—Teri Dutchman

"Christopher Harlan hit so close to home with this story. I don't think I could ever find the right words that will do justice for Away From Here because I'm actually speechless and pretty emotional about the story of Logan and Anna."

—Joann

DEDICATIONS

To Laylah, Holden, Serafina, and Frankie—the Club is no longer accepting applications. For you, this will just be a story, and no words can express how happy that makes me.

To the real Damien, whose name was Deron. Pete and I miss you.

To Alexandra, who appears as a little girl in the upper left hand corner of this cover in what's still one of my favorite pictures of my mom—thank you for helping me remember, and for offering your words at the end.

To Molly, Susan, and Pete—the last of those who knew the real people in this story.

To my other 'cover models' — Angelikh, Eleni, and Victoria —Iron, one and all.

As always, to my family for their support in this process.

And, finally, to the villains of this story, for reminding the heroes of why they exist.

AUTHOR'S NOTE—ON TRUTH AND FICTION

The crime that serves as the backbone of this narrative is true, and occurred on July 22ⁿᵈ, 1939, in an apartment complex that no longer stands, in the Bronx, New York. The victim was my great-grandmother and the perpetrator was my great-grandfather. This book is not a true crime retelling of that event, nor is it meant as a genealogical record of what happened afterwards. Like all fiction based on reality, there are blends of historical fact, truth and imagination. For all the reality that permeates the narrative, this isn't intended as historical record.

The essay that appears from Nathan's mom about midway through the story is an essay written by my mom, Victoria, as part of a writing competition she won after she went back to school at Queens College when I was a kid. Besides changing 'son' to 'children' for consistency purposes, I've left her award-winning story in her own voice, as it was meant to be read.

Above all, this is a story about the victims of victims, and the echoes of a ricochet that still pings from time to time. All of the events have been fictionalized, except, of course, for the ones that really happened—and all of the names of real people have been changed, except where I left them (mostly) the same.

Only a select few will know the difference.

—Christopher, 2019

FOREWORD

As I was about to send this off for final edits and formatting, while procrastinating on social media as I can sometimes do, I saw a post with a woman wearing a tee shirt that read "Strong women intimidate boys and excite men." This is true enough.

But it got me thinking—about how much of understanding, respecting, and loving the strength of women comes from the act of being raised by them. From knowing them. From loving them and witnessing their struggles first hand.

I was privileged in this way.

I'm honored to have borne witness to the things I saw, acknowledging that hindsight has cultivated that perspective.

But writing is remembering, and as I'm writing this foreword *after* I wrote the story you're about to read, I've reminded myself of something often lost in the haze of life— that I'm the benefactor of a long, storied, and often tragic history, and that is a gift, not a curse.

But in remembering, I've also come to a realization that needs articulation here.

There is no strong family without strong women. They are not only the foundation, but the earth on which the foundation lies; the material which builds ever upwards, and the sun which shines down upon the roof.

Strong women are the makers of history, and without the glow of their love we would all be lesser people.

This story is a tribute to those women who've come before.

Now it's my turn to raise one of my own.

My beautiful link in an unbroken chain.

THE SICK PARENTS CLUB

PART I

*". . .this is the only story in the world that nobody but me will
ever be able to tell."*

—Tana French, *In the Woods*

MY ATOMIC DREAMS

I went through this weird phase—one of many that characterized my adolescence—where I thought everything was going to explode. I didn't know the mechanism of the explosion, nor did I ever question it at the time. Maybe a bomb. Maybe a missile. Maybe just spontaneous combustion. I wasn't quite sure.

All I knew was that an end was coming, a cleansing that would rival the deepest Cold War atomic anxieties. Only my explosion wouldn't be an attack by a rival nation, intended to destroy everyone and everything. My explosion would be singular—surgical, as they say—intended for a target whose latitude and longitude aligned perfectly with my home and no one else's.

When the strike hit there would be panic, of course, followed by sadness and shock, and then the inevitable news cycle that would allow all the neighbors to give sound bites to local reporters about how kind we were, how we always helped shovel their snow when it got bad during those harsh New York winters, and what a shame it was that something so tragic had befallen such a nice family.

But strangely the blast never came. No explosion, no combustion, no chance for our shadows to fuse themselves into the ground like those poor bastards at Hiroshima, leaving a physical record of our tragedy for scientists to study. I just kept waking up, day after day, undestroyed by any external force.

But what troubled me the most wasn't the darkness of it all—not the fact that I was having such thoughts to begin with—but rather my inability to determine whether my atomic dreams were fear or fantasy—whether I was terrified of my family's imminent destruction, or if I sought the euthanasia of an already dying household.

OUR MAGIC BOX

Although I'd had my suspicions, the first time I knew for certain that I didn't come from a normal family was probably the day my sister and I went to visit our mom in a mental institution. We were five at the time.

I remember Dad laying out the nicest clothes that we owned, as though the other patients might judge us if we looked too ordinary. Clover yelled that nothing Dad picked out for her matched, which I'm sure it didn't, and she demanded to pick out her own outfit. He relented because, well, Clover was a strong-willed kid, and Dad probably didn't need the added stress her tantrum would have brought to an already stressful morning.

Before we left he pulled us into their room and told us to sit on the edge of their bed. That's when I knew it was serious —you only got to sit on the edge of your parents' bed for a talk when something major was happening. In our case, even though we wouldn't know the details until years later, he wanted us to know that our mom was very sick, and that sick people needed to be in a hospital so they could get better. That was meant to explain where Mom had been the past week, why she hadn't tucked us in at night, and why she hadn't been there for dinner. She was sick, he repeated, and the hospital was going to make her better.

Your mom made you something that she's going to give you at the hospital, he told us. It's something very special, and she made it just for you, with her very own hands. Do you know what it might be? Do you want to take a guess?

A magic box, Clover said, with far more certainty than she should have had at that moment. Dad's eyes widened like he'd seen a ghost. Yes, he told her. How did you know that? My sister just shrugged. It was yet another strange moment in a day that was strange by nature.

We visited Mom in the hospital a little bit later. We were confused because she didn't seem sick to us—she seemed like normal mom. She greeted us with hugs and kisses. We talked. We played. The orderlies watched over the whole thing like happy looking prison guards. And when our time was up, she said that she wanted to give us something and sat us down on the bench next to her. I made this for you, she told us. There's a special note inside of it for you, and it's a thing I want you to share. It belongs to both of you because it was made by me, and it's yours to have forever, long after I'm gone.

It's a magic box.

It's made for you to put things inside of—things that are important to you, things that are special. You can keep anything in there. Money, notes, keepsakes, even secrets.

Secrets? we asked.

Yes, even those. You can put things inside this box that you don't want anyone else to see, and they'll always be safe inside, no matter what.

The first thing I ever placed inside our magic box was the memory of that day, and when put inside it was mere wet clay

—crudely molded, barely holding its shape. But now, years later, as I pull it out of the box, it's fully solidified. It went in the memory of a child, but was retrieved as a metaphor for my mother: giving to others even when everyone had taken from her—creating things even as the disease inside was destroying her. The box was my family—odd and irrational in its existence, a keeper of secrets.

The greatest gift I've ever been given.

PART II

*"Each one fled at once—the moment the house committed
what was for him the one insult not to be borne or witnessed
a second time."*

—Toni Morrison, *Beloved*

A CURIOUS THING

The tapping of my fingers against computer keys is only perceptible after it ends. The silence that replaces the hour-long clicking session is an uncomfortable one because it allows me time to reflect on what I've written. I hate every word, as usual. We writers are our own worst critics, and sometimes with good cause.

But there's also a mild exuberance that rushes over me when I finish typing, mostly because the cessation of movement represents a finish line I always doubt my ability to cross. In this case it's an illusion—a false finish—the first of many.

I'd agreed to serialize the first few chapters of my next book for The New Yorker, a Faustian deal struck out of some deep seeded need to be different than other writers. Now I regret my hubris. I regret a lot about this project, but there's no going back now. The ink on the contract is dry. I'm writing this book no matter what.

The false finish was the end of my prologue, a document now waiting to be sent to the New Yorker with a simple click of my mouse. In typical fashion I hate every word I've written. That happens with every book, no matter how much positive feedback I get. My wife reassures me that this is just part of the process. Clover says the same. When two women you love and respect offer you the same piece of advice, it's best to listen. Still, it doesn't make me love the words I've written any more, even though I believe they're at least half respectable.

I attach the file to a cold sounding email text, thanking the editor of the magazine for taking an interest in my work, then hit the send button. It's done for now. The first finish line has been crossed, with many more to come.

I hear my wife's voice from behind me. "Are you still up?"

"You know I can never sleep when I'm on a deadline."

"I know," she says. "You just look exhausted."

"Uhh. . ." I groan. "Remind me again why I agreed to serialize this book."

"Because you're Nathan Dunbar, extraordinaire! *New York Times* and *Wall Street Journal* best selling author."

"You sound like the dust jacket of one of my books" I joke back. "But, seriously, I don't know what I was thinking."

Time was, not too long ago, that both of us would stay up until three a.m. watching TV and talking, but pregnancy's changed more than a few dynamics between us. That isn't a complaint—quite the contrary. The sight of our baby growing inside of her is the most miraculous thing anyone has ever experienced in the history of the world. That's how it feels anyhow. But having a person inside of you also means frequent trips to the bathroom, sickness that transcends the confines of morning hours, and nodding off to sleep around lights out at the local old age home. Tonight seems to be an exception to that last part.

"Not going well, I take it. How can I help?"

"I hate it," I blurt out.

"Your book?"

"It's not even a book yet. It's a prologue of questionable quality for readers that aren't even my core audience."

"Then why are you writing it?"

The 'it' in question isn't just my book. The 'it' is the story I've been trying to tell since long before I decided to try my hand at being a published author—the story of my great grandmother's murder.

"Shitty decision making, I guess. But there's no going back now."

"I'm no writer, but I can't imagine hating what you're doing is going to make for a good book."

She's right. Even though there's nothing I can do about it now. "Can you read it?" I ask. "Maybe I'm doing that self-deprecating thing that you and Clover always tell me I do."

"We have this talk at least once a book, don't we? And of course I'll read it. Give me ten minutes."

"Okay, I'll leave. I'll grab a snack out of the fridge while you read."

"Actually, hold that thought." I furrow my brow, not sure where she's going with this. "How about you read it to me?"

"Read it to you? Like, out loud?"

"Yeah, why not? You used to read to me all the time before your first book came out. Remember?"

It's one of my fondest memories of a time that I wasn't otherwise fond of. It was twelve years ago, a time before I knew my literary ass from my elbow. I had just signed the first of many contracts, gotten a decent advance from my publishing company, and had to deal with the pressure of having to live up to all of the expectations that came with it.

I worked my butt off, every night, no matter how shitty the pages smelled, until I had something that resembled a real life novel. When the hard parts came—and they came in legions—I always read them aloud to her. She'd tell me they were great, that I was just being insecure because it was my first novel, and her reassurances gave me the confidence I so desperately needed at the time. I need that magic again.

"Here," I say, getting up from my chair so that she can sit. "Just let me print out a copy, a book shouldn't be read off of a screen." I reopen the file and hit the print button, and once the pages come out I sit down and look at what I've written, the words still fresh in my mind, ready to read to my wife.

An Excerpt from the upcoming novel "*Ricochet: The Dark Story of My Family's History*" by New York Times bestselling author Nathan Dunbar

A bullet is a curious thing.

It isn't intended to multi-task, but rather to accomplish a solitary purpose—to fly at imperceptible speeds, through time and space, and to destroy its intended target. In this way they're wonderfully simple, uncomplicated in design and purpose, waiting only to be loaded into a chamber and released. But they're also unpredictable, as all objects meant only to destroy can be, and once freed from the darkness of their chamber they can do things both unexpected and unintended.

The bullet that was let loose in the early morning hours of July 22nd, 1939, was not intended to strike down an enemy in war, nor to defend a life. It was not meant to liberate or protect. It was released with the intent of completing a job for which the shooter's disease-riddled brain informed him he was uniquely qualified.

That job, carried out with a military-like precision, was to end the life of the woman who had been his wife of several decades, the mother of his five children, and my great grandmother. Her name was Angelikh—Angela, in English—and, at the time she was gunned down in front of her children, she was forty-seven years old.

The man, whose name was Thomas, believed himself justified. It was simply a matter of retribution for the wrongs his wife had committed, namely her believed infidelity with countless, nameless men, who Thomas' sick thoughts repeatedly reminded him existed.

Like many women struck down by those they love, her only true crime was marrying a man who would eventually murder her; which Thomas did with a single shot from a 22 caliber handgun that was ironically kept in the home for protection. While tragic, his actions that morning were hardly original. He had threatened or tried to kill Angela several times before actually doing so. What followed everyone's denial of those warning signs was the inevitable end to such a story.

The only direct witness to the slaughter, my grandmother, would later recall how she'd warned her mother repeatedly about Thomas' increasingly erratic and violent behavior; how she tried to inform the police, and how, tragically, no one would listen to the silly concerns of an immigrant girl like her. This fact would haunt her the rest of her life. In later years she would also remark that, of all the shocks she received that day, she never realized what a bullet could do to a human body; how something so small could flip the off switch to an entire entity, with the effortless squeeze of a finger.

My own shock came in the realization that a bullet could destroy an entire family; that it could ricochet with such precision through generations not yet born. I likewise never realized that a bullet has an essence, just as a person does. And, like a person, long after the physical form has departed, that essence can still manifest from time to time, showing up like a ghost, to do what bullets are meant to do.

I can't be angry at them for this. Like the wasp, stinging victims again and again with the impunity not afforded the bee, a bullet just does what is essential for it to do. They are the slave. It's the master who we need to direct our ire towards; the one who gives the bullet its intent.

Or maybe men like Thomas, stricken with murderous insanity, can be held no more accountable for his actions than the mindless piece of lead that his finger released that day. Perhaps he too was set on a path, long before the events of that morning, in ways no one can ever know or understand. And, like the bullet leaving its chamber, once he was set on that path, only a singular outcome was ever possible.

While explanatory, I have to remind myself that explanation is not tantamount to forgiveness, and that I must not take such historically distant analysis to its logical end. There is such a thing as too much understanding.

I do have to wonder though, having lived with the

residue of that morning my entire life—was it all inevitable? Could Angela have married a better man? Could Thomas have abstained from the very types of infidelities he believed his wife guilty of, and not contracted a disease that would eventually rob him of his mind? Could my grandmother have done a better job of convincing her mother that Thomas was, in fact, losing more of his sanity with each passing sunrise, and that the best course of action was having him committed?

Questions with insufficient answers—one and all. But, still, I have to wonder, even if no true answers are ever afforded me. Can a ricocheting bullet, like the one that destroyed my family, ever be silenced? Can it, like an angry poltergeist that mindlessly haunts a home, one day be exorcised, until only the silence of peace remains?

I don't know.

But inside these pages you'll find the story of that crime, as best as I can tell it.

THE SMELL OF SPENT GUNPOWDER
FILLING MY NOSE

When I finish I'm proud and embarrassed at the same time, a hybrid of emotions I'm not quite sure what to do with.

"It's good," she tells me. I don't know how to feel about that compliment. We used to have this running joke between us. I'd make fun of her anytime she referred to someone as nice. What a terrible thing to say, I'd tell her. When she looked at me, puzzled, I'd explain that 'nice' wasn't a compliment, it was a thing we called people when we had nothing better to say about them. Everyone's nice, I told her, it's like saying someone has two eyes — perfectly obvious and perfectly ordinary. That's how writers feel about the word good.

"It's good, huh? That's exactly what I was afraid of."

"Oh, come on, don't go sensitive writer on me, you know what I meant."

She looks at me lovingly, like what she's about to say will both sting a little and be necessary for me to hear. I brace myself for the criticism. "You know how I feel about your words. They're beautiful. Palaces out of paragraphs, right?"

I smile at her reference. Hamilton is our show—we saw it

earlier in the year through some connections my agent had; otherwise we never would have been able to get our hands on tickets. The show is everything that everyone said it was; brilliant, inspirational, touching, and original, like almost nothing else on Broadway I've ever seen. But it was the emphasis on Hamilton's writing—a recurring theme throughout the show, that I really attached to. Ever since then my wife finds ways to work in little quotes from the show into our lives. Tonight it's to subtlety let me know that I'm capable of more than what I've just put on the page.

"You know that line is from a song about her hating him for cheating, right?"

"I know," she answers. "But it was the right line for the moment. I don't want you to burn, I promise."

"I appreciate that."

We laugh. The feeling of my belly rising and falling chases the doubt away momentarily.

"It's what I'm here for. But I wasn't finished just yet, you know."

"I know," I answer. "It was just nice to take my mind off this for a second."

"This isn't like you."

"What?"

"Being so self loathing—so self deprecating. You seem like you're not loving what you're doing."

Hearing her say what I've been thinking for a while now allows me to experience the sentiment without guilt. I'm not loving what I'm doing, and I'm not accustomed to my job feeling like work.

"I'm like Sisyphus, perpetually moving that fucking rock."

"You're like a dramatic author, is what you are. Jesus,

20

Nate, you just went Greek mythology on me. You're just having some kind of block."

"No, see, that's the thing. It's not a block at all. The idea is there, the framework is all sketched out. The words are flowing like cheap booze on St. Patty's Day."

"Holy crap, Nate. One more metaphor or simile and I'm taking the baby and moving far, far away. You're killing me, Smalls."

"Sorry," I say. "Force of habit. Writer stuff."

"How many chapters do you owe the magazine?"

"I've committed to three, but we're still negotiating the possibility of more if I wanted to."

"Okay, good. So, first things first—you don't want to do any more than that. You get your money and they get their agreed upon three chapters. Nothing more or less. And you can bang out three chapters in your sleep, am I right?" I nod. I love her confidence in me. "Right. Then that's all you'll do. You can renegotiate with your publishing company after that."

"Renegotiate?" I ask, confused. "For what?"

"To have those three chapters be an extra."

Now I'm really confused. "An extra for?"

"For the real book," she says, her eyes fixed and intense. "The one you're really trying to write but don't seem to realize."

"What are you talking about? What book?"

"The one about the Club. The story that only you can tell."

That's when the full impact of her words reach somewhere deep inside of me that I'd long since buried. Like a wave, the past crashes over me, and the images flash before me. The Back. The Club. All of it. A kaleidoscopic slide show plays itself in real time, and the stories whisper into my ears.

She squeezes my shoulder again. I look down. The flatness of her belly has been replaced with the bump that holds my unborn daughter, keeping her protected until she's ready to greet this world. As I gaze at her swollen belly, the future and the past blend into a seamless hybrid, becoming so interwoven that they're impossible to disentangle.

"You know I haven't even said her name out loud in years. Not until I just read it to you."

"Angela?" she asks.

I nod again. "Yeah. I've wanted to tell her story for so long. Maybe that's the real reason I agreed to this insanity with The New Yorker."

She places a gentle hand on my arm, and the warmth of her skin against mine focuses me. "How can you tell her story without telling yours and your mom's?"

My wife's a teacher—third grade—and like any good teacher she asks the right questions to get the responses that matter. And in this case there's only one answer. "I can't." I pause for a moment. "Do you remember when we talked about ghosts? Do you remember what we said to one another?"

"I remember every word. Don't you?"

"I think so," I tell her. "I have this theory that there's no such thing as forgetting, and that what we call forgetting is just a way for our brains to file things away, like old papers in a drawer. Sometimes the drawer is locked. Sometimes you just can't find the key. The word we chose for that is forgetting."

"You're such a writer," she laughs. "And you should call your sister to get her take on the book. She was there, you know?"

22

"A lot of people were there," I joke, looking her in the eye. "Should I have them all contribute?"

"Only the ones you share genetic material with. And now I'm officially up too late. This pregnant lady is going to sleep."

"I'll be there soon. Don't wait for me."

She laughs hysterically. "That's a good one. Are you going to write tonight?"

"Maybe," I say. We both know my maybe means yes.

"Remember what your mom always said to you."

"What?"

"*Say that thing with which you labor*," she reminds me. "Now don't stay up too late."

I watch my wife and unborn baby leave the room, and that quote rings in my ears. Thoreau. My mom loved Thoreau. And that's when the full realization hits me. The story of Angela isn't a true crime novel, it's a metaphor for the collective story of the women in my family. What happened to her effected every person who lived after her, myself included. And there's no way to tell her story without telling our story—of The Meadows, the Club, and the day that Serafina went missing.

I decide to call my sister. She picks up by the third ring.

"I was just thinking of you," she says.

"I wish everyone answered the phone like that," I joke. "What are you working on?"

"At the moment I'm working on getting Chase to brush his teeth before bed, but it's not going so well. I swear making the Times was easier than being a mom sometimes."

My sister and I are both successful authors. It's not something either of us take for granted, even though if you heard us talking about making the *New York Times* so casually we'd sound like total snobs.

"You're making parenthood sound so appealing."

"Oh, don't be a wimp. You're not the one pushing a watermelon sized creature out of your vagina."

"This is true," I say, laughing. "I guess that's your way of saying that things could be worse."

"It's my way of telling you to keep perspective."

"You have a way with words, Clover."

"So I've been told," she jokes. "So what's going on? To what do I owe the call?" I hear her six-year-old son, Chase, yelling 'no teeth' in the background so loudly that it sounds like he's the one I'm on the phone with. I want to laugh except that I know one day I'll be the one chasing a little one around the house with a toothbrush.

"I have an idea I wanted to run by you, but I'm not sure how you'll respond."

"Well good thing I'm here to let you know. Try me."

My sister has a complicated relationship with our past, which is to say that she has a complicated relationship with the truth. To her it's a thing to be forgotten—moved on from—something that need never be discussed in much depth past the factual recall of things. And on those we agree: we grew up in Queens, New York. We lived in a residential neighborhood called the Meadows. We had a small group of friends that were like family. And we came from a very not normal family.

It's the other journalism questions—the whys and hows—where our interpretations diverge. I've spent the last few decades of my life trying to understand; to find meaning; to discover what I can about my family's history. Clover would rather not talk about it.

I tell her what I plan on doing now that my wife has given me the push I so desperately needed. I'm going to write a book, I tell her. It's going to be about our great grandmother's murder, but really its going to be about us. Our home. Mom and Dad. Carmine, Damien and Serafina. The Back. All of it.

"I think it's a great idea," she tells me after a pause so long that I was expecting the opposite reaction.

"Really? That's great!"

"You didn't expect me to say that, did you?"

"Not really, no. But I'm glad you did. I have a favor though."

"Ask away."

"Will you beta read for me once I have a real first draft? I need you to be okay with what's inside before I publish it. I need your feedback."

"I'd be honored, Nate, you know that. Whatever you need."

Actually, Clover, I didn't know that. I thought you'd laugh. I thought at the least you'd make up some excuse to not be able to read what I'm going to write — a deadline, kid stuff, whatever. But you surprise me every once in a blue moon.

"Great," I tell her. "I'll let you know when I'm done. Good luck with the tooth brushing thing. I'm sure I'll be there one day."

"Before you know it, Nate the Great. Before you know it. Night."

"Night."

Once we're off the phone I get right down to business. My wife knows me too well. I should be going to bed—resting up so I can finish my last few chapters, but I have things I need to get out. It's time to let my fingers do the remembering.

I open a new file, and the words flow from me as though they'd already been written.

I'd never seen a ghost before that night—wasn't even sure they existed.

Sure, I'd heard all the stories. We all had. Local ones, too, like that business over in Amityville, Long Island. That was only an hour from where I grew up—even less if the Long Island Expressway wasn't jammed with traffic. But let's face it, the LIE was always jammed with traffic.

Those people over in Long Island saw demonic pigs, swarms of flies in winter, and the kinds of things that still have teenagers driving by the house every weekend to gawk. But it turns out all that ghost stuff was a hoax, some bullshit to sell books and make a hit movie. The real Amityville horror was something even darker, something much more human.

Before stories of ghosts and demons, there was a family by the name of Defeo that lived in the house. Two parents and five kids—two sisters and three brothers. The oldest boy, Ronald, took a rifle and wiped out his entire family, one by one, in the autumn of 1974. It was one of the worst murder cases of the decade, maybe ever. It wasn't talking pig heads that haunted that house in Amityville, it was the stain of a crime so terrible that it stuck, like bad wallpaper that won't come off clean; working its way into the very fibers of the place. Angela was murdered like the Defeo's; her children awoken by gunfire, just like those poor sleeping kids.

The photos will help me remember her. It's been years since I've looked at any of them, but when I open the file on my computer there she is, frozen in sepia, the picture saying everything and nothing all at once. The first file that opens is only her, her face docile and delicate, turned left and slightly upwards, as though instructed by the photographer. The next is of the whole family. Baby grandmother is sitting in the middle, surrounded by baby great uncles and aunts. Everyone is smiling.

Memories are tricksters, and photographs are liars. As I get ready to lay down next to my pregnant wife and close my eyes, I'm a kid again, transported back to my room where Angela sat and extended her hand to me.

I'll never forget the way the ghost of my great grandmother looked, sitting in my room like it was nothing, her face calm and pale, her eyes remembering everything. Those eyes. Brown so dark they looked black, and filled with history. Our history. I'll never forget that sound—the one she brought with her. The faint pinging, over and over, in the background, and the smell of spent gunpowder filling my nose.

THREE MONTHS LATER

A neighborhood is a character, not a setting.

They have histories all their own, just like the individuals who occupy their geographies. And it's within their borders that the story of a community takes place. By the time I was eighteen I used college as an excuse to leave the neighborhood I grew up in—those handful of blocks that once held all the majesty and wonder of childhood, but by that point had become the place I needed to get away from. My twin sister Clover did the same. Mom stayed for the rest of her life.

Now I'm back, at least for a visit. I don't know why I asked Clover to meet me here. We could have talked about the book at my place on the Island, or hers in the city, or anywhere else in between, really. But something was calling me back home.

Today it's a hot one, and the type of hot that makes it impossible to concentrate on anything except the inescapable feeling of discomfort that surrounds you. Sweat starts to drip almost immediately, in places unaccustomed to such wetness. It reminds me of that one hot yoga class my wife dragged me to a few years back when we were dating. I never knew that a body could leak like that. I have that same feeling as my feet hit the ground for the first time in years.

The Meadows.

Being back on these streets is like a lucid dream — the feeling of surreal blends seamlessly with the feeling of hyper awareness. Before meeting Clover, I decide to make one quick stop. As I abandon the comfort of my car's air conditioning and step into a humid July afternoon, all the feelings I haven't felt in years come flooding back to me. It's strange how geography can impact your emotions. I put on my sunglasses to block the oppressive rays bearing down on me, and take my first steps down 71st Crescent in well over a decade.

Outwardly not much is different than I remember. Two-story duplexes sit in linear rows, attached to one another down the length of the block, each adorned with its own little square lawn that's barely big enough to plant anything in. Mostly they're for show. A small concrete mold holds a place for the garbage cans adjacent to the tiny yards, and two short concrete steps form stoops that lead to front doors. I look around and take a deep breath.

I haven't been here since Mom died two years ago. Cancer. Does anyone die of anything else anymore? Dad went a few years before her, leaving our childhood home occupied with people I'll never know, forging their own memories without any knowledge of what happened inside those walls. I suppose that's the natural order of things, but seeing it in person feels strange.

As I approach our duplex—which we now each refer to as Mom's Place in some strange disconnect from the fact that we grew up there—I see Mrs. Gennison weeding in what must be the smallest garden in the world. If it's possible she looks younger now than I remember her when I was a kid, but she still has that flaming orange hair that signifies to the world that you're a little off. A normal person would have read the box at CVS better to gauge the color. A normal person, even having not read the box properly, would have screamed in horror after wiping the steam off of their bathroom mirror to reveal a head of hair like Pennywise the Clown.

I doubt any of her friends or relatives bother to tell her how textbook a case of obsessive-compulsive disorder she has. I doubt she ever saw a therapist for it. People of her generation mostly thought of Psychology as a sort of social science version of a Yeti sighting or an alien abduction story — something a few nutty people believed in and swore by, yet something reasonable people didn't put much stock in. *No*, she'd probably think, *I just like things in their place— organized, orderly, what's so wrong with that?*

I remember watching her from the middle upstairs bedroom, voyeuristic little shit that I could be back then, her OCD in full manifestation, like my own private show, as she checked every door of her car, one at a time, to make sure it was locked. She'd repeat that cycle exactly seven times, every day, without fail. If only she'd known about my counting all those years ago—we could have bonded over our mutual compulsions. Hindsight's a bitch.

I wave politely and smile as I walk by. I stop outside of our old place for just a minute—just long enough to remember, and then I get back in my car. The old Starbucks is calling my name, and knowing Clover she's at least a Cappuccino ahead of me already.

When I get there about ten minutes later my suspicions are proven correct. I see her in the window seat, her head angled back, the bottom of her cup held high. I walk in and wave. She sees me right away, and the spent cup on the table confirms my suspicions. "I knew it."

"What?" she asks.

"That you'd be here already. That's Clover, always punctual."

"And that's Nathan, always late." I see a second cup at the end of the table, adjacent to her.

"Touché. You ordered for me?"

"Twin thing. I know my brother."

I grab my coffee and take a sip. "Thank you."

"You got it. I can't believe you actually finished. I almost fell out of bed when you texted me the other night."

It's true, I wrote an entire book in two months. I've been fine tuning the drafts for the past few weeks. The words poured out of me, but it still needs more editing, a cover, and all the other things that a book needs before it's finished. But what it needs most of all—the validation that I'm seeking most of all—is Clover's seal of approval. She was generous enough with her time to read the draft I'd written, and the whole idea of this meeting is to get her feedback from a writer's standpoint. She takes a deep breath and looks at me like she's stressed by the prospect of discussing things from our past.

"My therapist wasn't sure if this process was going to be good for me."

"Well did you tell Dr. Whatever to fuck off? That this is something involving your family that you need to be a part of?"

"I didn't put it quite that way, but yes, I did. He was just concerned about me, Nate."

My sister's been in therapy since just before she published her first book. If you asked her, she'd tell you that it's like pre-emptive care given all the mental health issues in our family. "I'm just getting ahead of the curve," she'd confessed to me when she started going. "If all the women in our family died of breast cancer, you wouldn't judge me for getting regular mammograms, would you? It's the same thing."

"I don't judge you at all," I told her. "I didn't judge Mom and Dad either, that was always your thing."

The last part was a little bit of a dig, but it was also the truth. Sometimes the two overlap. I didn't really think that her therapy was pre-emptive care, no matter how much she repeated that tired, rehearsed qualification. I always suspected that she was suffering from something and needed help. Two years ago, on Thanksgiving, we were all together at my place —me, my wife, and Clover and her husband—when she asked me if I could grab the copy of her new novel she'd brought from her bag. When I reached over to hand her the bag my hand slipped, and all of her stuff rolled every which direction on the floor. I felt terrible, so I put down the dish I was carrying and started picking her stuff back up despite her protest that she could do it. The first item that found its way into my hand was a prescription bottle for Clonazepam.

"It's really okay, Nathan, I can get it."

I could tell by her tone that she didn't want me to know that she was on meds for anxiety, so I pretended like I didn't read the label when I handed it back to her. "You have that upper respiratory thing again?" The speed at which I covered up the truth for her benefit was impressive.

"Yeah," she lied. "Throat's been killing me."

"It's going around. Make sure you finish the whole bottle or it can come back even stronger."

"Yup," she said nervously. "That's what my doctor said. You missed your calling."

The memory ends and I'm pulled back into the present.

33

"I'm glad you wrote this book, Nate. I know you don't believe me. It's something I never could have done myself."

"It's almost something I didn't do." I snicker, but it's one of those socially contrived laughs—the combination of snort and laugh you make when you don't want to say something too serious, so you pretend there's humor in your statement when there really isn't. "It was a lot of work. But I think I have something there."

"All your books are great, this one included. I know it's not totally finished yet, but I loved what I read."

"Its greatness is yet to be determined." I stop because I don't know how to say what I need to say to her. The real reason I came here isn't just to get her opinion on the draft of the book. I have ulterior motives. There were specific parts of the book that I wanted her to read—my confession about things I never told her when we were kids. She hasn't mentioned those parts, and committing them to paper was my passive aggressive way of confessing to her. We need to talk about it, and it can't be sitting here in a crowded Starbucks. "Idea," I say, faking a cheery smile.

"What's that? Another book idea?"

"No," I joke. "I think I'm all good with writing for a few weeks, at least. I was thinking we get seconds because, well, we both love caffeine."

"I'm with you so far."

"And then I was thinking we get out of here and do a little sight seeing. Take an overly caffeinated tour down memory lane."

"Okay," she says hesitantly. "How come?"

"I don't know. The book has me feeling nostalgic. I wrote everything from memory. I was just thinking it was a nice day outside and we're not over here often. I'd like to walk around, catch up a little."

It's strange that all of what I just told her is true, yet it's simultaneously a complete lie. I am feeling nostalgic, and it is a beautiful day. I love walks, and I love to take them while sipping on a drink. But my real motivation is finding a place that we can talk without being interrupted or distracted. And I think I know just the place.

"Sure. That sounds nice. Where'd you have in mind?"

"The Grove," I tell her, and so quickly it's hard to hide the fact that I'd already had this planned. "Let's go to the Oak Grove. It's time to remember."

PART III

THE SICK PARENTS CLUB (1996)

". . .I was beginning to learn that your life is a story told about you, not one that you tell."

—John Green, *Turtles All the Way Down*

"We don't fall in love with the perfect person; we fall in love despite a person's imperfections."

— Vi Keeland, *We Shouldn't*
@vi_keeland, www.vikeeland.com

"I'm fascinated by the ways in which we all view, experience, and hold our trauma. . .Surviving is more than just fodder for content."

—Jessamyn Stanley (www.jessamynstanley.com /

@mynameisjessamyn, @theunderbellyyoga, @jessamyntwerks, #everybodyyoga).

THE VICTIMS OF VICTIMS

Our family was not normal. Not at all. Not even a little bit.

Best to establish that right at the beginning of the story.

This sounds very cliche, I realize, because, who in their right mind believes their family normal? No one I know, and probably no one you know either. But I'd argue that there are degrees of normal—a sliding scale of sorts, where 1 is some *Leave-It-To-Beaver*-like experience had by no one outside of a Hollywood script, and 10 is like that family of cannibals from *Texas Chainsaw Massacre*. I don't know where we fell on that continuum, but we sure as hell weren't normal.

My parents weren't bad people, they were just the victims of victims—my made-up term for the people who are recyclers of their own emotional damage. My parents fit that mold to a T—so much so that even as a teenager I was capable of at least understanding, if not forgiving, why they were the way they were.

I'd love to sit here and chronicle the atrocities of my parents' collective youths so that you could understand them better, but the fact is that the atrocities of youth don't get their own genealogist. Those things happen in the shadows; behind slammed doors, in the quietest of places where their evil can be trapped and sealed in. To tell you the honest truth, I wish I had those stories to tell, but I don't. Kids don't get those stories, we just get to live with the results. And that's what I can tell you about—that's what me and my friends were experts in—being the children of the victims of victims.

I had this very conversation with my best friend Carmine one time. Actually, he had it with me.

"My parents could care less what happens to me," he told me, all dramatic and angry.

"What are you talking about?"

"After we hung out yesterday, I walked around the neighborhood for a while. I was trying to be late."

"Why were you trying to be late?"

"Let's call it an experiment, okay? Like Mr. Briggs taught us about in Bio. I was testing a hypothesis."

"Which was?"

"That unlike ninety-nine percent of the kids we know, I could walk into my place an hour late, miss family dinner, and not have anyone bat an eye. They didn't even ask where I was. Don't you find that a little weird?"

Carmine was one of seven. His parents were pulling numbers like you'd expect in a forth world tribal society or a fundamentalist Mormon compound. They were old school Italians, hence the name, and he was the runt of the litter, the 'oops' baby who was never allowed to forget the fact that he owed his existence to a bottle of grappa and a mistimed pullout. Because of this, Carmine was one of the few kids I knew who actually craved more rules and regulations in his life. His dream was to be grounded for some dumb shit that would have annoyed the rest of us. The grass was always greener.

"I'm telling you, man, no one gives a single fuck about me."

He got worked up like that at least once a month, always over how his folks treated him, and there was never any talking him out of it, even though I still tried. That was Best Friendship 101, first lecture.

"Look man, I'm sure that's not true. We've talked about this."

"Oh Jesus, I don't even know why I tell you these things."

"Cause I'm your best friend, and that's what you do with best friends—you tell them things. What else is there?"

"Yeah, I guess. I just feel misunderstood."

"Get in line."

Carmine's real issue wasn't just that he was neglected, but *why* he was neglected. There was the unfortunate birth order thing, but there wasn't anything he could do about that. The real problem was his father. Three separate tours in Vietnam had left Carmine's dad a little south of well-adjusted. He was like a character in an Oliver Stone film, with every symptom of PTSD checked off. He was angry most days, erratic, prone to violence, and unpredictable in his moods. That left my bestie in a position where he went back and forth between wanting his parents' attention and fearing when he got it. It wasn't that his parents didn't love him, or that they were too tired at this point in their lives to parent, they were just tired in general, and too messed up to care what their seventh kid was doing in science class.

"It's different," Carmine said. "I know you're going to do your therapy thing right now, right? Explain away all the shit that makes my parents the way they are? Now I know why Clover always gets pissed at you."

What he was referring to was my weird ability, even back then, to put myself in the mindset of others. Some kids were good at baseball, others at doing geometry. I was good at being empathetic. Normally this would have been a good thing, except for the fact that I could understand bad people's motivations also. What everyone got wrong—my friends, my sister, everyone—is that my ability to explain where someone was coming from wasn't the same as me agreeing with them or forgiving the bad things they'd done.

"Fine," I said, not wanting to get into it. "I won't do my therapy thing. You're right, your parents are terrible people. They hate you, and you'll be fucked up for the rest of your days because of it. I'm sorry I said otherwise."

"Don't be a dick."

"It's hard sometimes."

Carmine laughed. "That's what she said!"

Then I laughed. I was mature, but I was still a teenaged boy. "I set that up nicely for you, didn't I?"

"Perfectly. I appreciate it."

"Anytime," I said. "But look, man, I'm not making excuses for your parents. If you say they don't care then maybe they don't—or maybe they're bad at letting you know they care, I don't know. But either way, they're your parents. We only get two. Gotta make the best of it."

"Like you and your dad?" he asked.

"Different story," I said.

Carmine knew he'd get a reaction out of me with that one. My one blind spot was my father. We didn't get along. Like chocolate and eggs, we were fine when taken on our own merits, but about as shitty a pair as you could combine.

"Right," he said back. "Always a different story. Whatever, man. Let's talk about something else."

"Fine. How about Damien's outfit today?"

"Man, that kid's uncoordinated as all fuck. Looks like a

blind person went on a shopping spree at five different stores and just put random shit all over his body."

"I know!"

Clover and I didn't have neglectful parents like Carmine. I don't know what kind of parents we had. I guess classifications were stupid, but what we both knew from a young age was that, although equally fucked up, Mom and Dad were different animals. Mom was a parent, while Dad was just kind of there.

She'd raised us like a single parent even though she was very much married to our father. Dude had a gift for being absent even when he was present. It was as though he'd decided at some point that he was done—done with being a husband, sure as fuck done with being a father, and was generally content to be one of those guys who punched the clock, ate a mostly unhealthy dinner, then zombified himself with some prime-time TV before nodding off around ten.

When Clover and I inquired as to why Dad was so terrible at said position (with those 'what the fuck, Mom' looks we'd shoot her when he didn't want to talk, or ask us about school, or generally want to know about anything going on in our lives) she'd tell us he was just tired. That was her go-to. Motherfucker sure was tired a lot. That was her coping mechanism for having to explain to two young children why their dad didn't seem to care much about them.

These questions didn't go away. All that changed were Mom's excuses. When we were in middle school it transitioned from 'he's tired' (this was due to Clover, being her precocious self, suggesting to Mom that if Dad was so damn tired all the time, there must be a medical issue, and that she should take him to the doctor and report the results to us immediately) to being 'it's complicated, guys.'

Being old enough to question these things, albeit gently, we pushed back on anything that wreaked of parental bullshit. What does that mean? Complicated how? What's complicated about a father who doesn't care?

I've got to give it to Mom, she navigated those waters as best as she could for as long as she could, but after a while those kinds of questions demanded answers, and eventually she broke. I got so sick of Dad's bullshit and neglect that I started asking the same questions Clover always asked, but for some reason when I asked I got answers.

So what the fuck, Mom? I know, I shouldn't have cursed, but that's how sick I was of being raised in a single parent household even though I had two parents. Finally, she told me what I had always suspected deep down all along, though how I knew of such things I couldn't tell you. It was his past, baby. It isn't you, he loves you both more than anything in the world.

What about his past? I asked.

That's when Mom tried to offer an explanation—as if there was such a thing—for why Dad wasn't much of one. I insisted Clover be there, she needed to hear this crap also. But I loved Mom and knew this wasn't her fault, outside of her marrying this man, so I gave her the respect to at least listen.

He was the oldest of three, she explained. You two wouldn't understand that because you're twins, but birth order matters. Your father had to take care of his brother and sister because his dad—your grandfather—was a drunk. You don't remember this, but he died of sclerosis (that's a liver disease only alcoholics get, she explained). His mom had her own problems. So that left your father to raise his siblings. I think by the time he became an actual father he was just tired.

There is was.

An explanation that both was and wasn't. It existed. It made some degree of psychological sense. But it was also nothing—excuse of all excuses; something to be told to a therapist later in life when he asked your sister why she had relationship issues and always went after the wrong men. Because, Mr. Therapist, my dad was too tired to raise me because he raised his brother and sister instead, decades before I was born. See you next week.

I think we just stared at Mom after she said that. I have to give it to her, took some balls to actually tell your kids their dad was in a state of semi-retirement from all fatherly duties. I don't know what happened before or after—don't recall what I had for lunch, or what TV shows I viewed before letting my head hit the pillow that night. But what I do remember is that was the night I realized what a Victim of Victims is. Knowing me, I probably just nodded and said okay. I never liked adding to Mom's misery. More on that shortly. Clover probably just stared, looking resentful. That was her favorite outfit.

But the purpose of that little anecdote wasn't just to tell you about our dad. Really, it was to tell you about our mom. Let me make an objective statement, even though it'll sound the opposite of that. Just gonna have to take my word on this one as your trusted narrator. My mom was the strongest person I've ever known, hands down, bar none. But mostly when I describe her I'm gonna make her sound weak as hell. It's the irony of depression and anxiety. It reduces you to a coward, it robs you of who you really are, it takes your strength and feasts on your energy. But surviving it makes you the strongest person in the world, even if you look like you're only a mild gust of wind from blowing away forever.

I used to wonder where it all started.

With superheroes—like Spectacular Spider-Man or Wolverine (two of my closest friends when I was a kid), they called it an origin story, the way mild mannered (Whoever) became the hero in the panels I loved to read. I mean, who didn't know about Bruce Wayne's parents getting killed by a robber in that alley? Who wasn't familiar with Peter Parker being bitten by a radioactive spider, and his failure to stop the guy who killed his Uncle Ben (. . .with great power. . .)? As the years went on, I started to wonder what my family's origin story was, or if anyone even knew.

"Clover, do you know anything about Mom or Dad?"

"Can you ask that in a better way?"

"Like, do you know anything about them before they were Mom and Dad? When they were just people."

"They're still people, stupid."

"You know what I mean."

"I really, really don't. That's the problem."

"God, you can be difficult! I mean, do you know anything about Mom and Dad's lives before us?"

"We both know some stuff. What do you want to know?"

"I guess not just about them, but about how they grew up. Mom, specifically. Like, what happened in her life to make her like she is now."

"It's called Depression, stupid. You know that as well as I do. We know it better than Mom's therapists."

She was right about that. Depression was one of those words we shouldn't have known about—like 'psychosis', 'clinical', and other terms that no one outside of a first-year psychology student or kid with severely messed up parents would know. We were the latter, so we knew shit that was probably better not to know. I don't recall a pre-depression Mom or a pre-psychosis Dad. They existed—of this I was certain—but I was unaware of how they came to be the Mom and Dad that we knew.

One night I finally found out, when Mom told me about the family's deep dark secret, the thing no one would speak of outside of closed bedroom doors—our very own radioactive spider.

THE MURDER

It started, as most things did back then, with tears.

Really a faint sobbing; unmistakable in its perfect melody of shallow breaths and faintly uttered sadness. I'd heard it before a million times over because, well, that's what happened in our house. Mom cried. It was as predictable as the sunset, as disquieting as a hail storm against the roof in the middle of the night. The sounds didn't affect me like they used to when I was younger because I heard them so often that they just became background noise—as common as the coffee machine spitting out steaming hot blackness, or the squeaking of my front door when it opened.

There was one night in particular. Banal as it got. Nothing extraordinary except for what followed the gentle rapping of my knuckles against her closed bedroom door. The invitation to come in presented itself that night, hidden behind a shaky voice. I took it, not knowing exactly what I could even do to help. It didn't matter. Clover was out, Dad was out. That left me, and that was all the reasoning the situation required.

When I went inside mom was on her bed, blanket

wrapped around her small, frail body, and only a single light —the dim lamp that sat on her nightstand—was on. I jumped on the bed and hugged her because that was what made sense to do. She hugged me back, and after some small talk she began the story, as though she'd been waiting my entire life to reveal it to me.

Did I ever tell you about your great-grandmother?

The one in the pictures?

Yes. The black and whites. The one cradling my mother when she was still a baby. That one.

She was beautiful.

Yes, she was. Did I ever tell you what happened to her?

No. I don't think you did. She died a long time ago, right?

A very long time ago. She was murdered. She was killed by a man who should have protected her.

I remember not speaking much after she said that. What the hell was there to say except, my god—lower case 'g' because I had recently discovered atheism, and it was more expression than declaration of faith. She continued despite my shock.

That's right. My grandmother, your great grandmother, was murdered in front of my mother, your grandmother. Shot in the head. Shot by her husband.

The Murder—that's what she called it, definite article for emphasis. No one likes to talk about the Murder, she told me. None of your great aunts or uncles, none of your cousins. It's the Queen Bee of dark family secrets, and even though it shaped us for generations, no one likes to acknowledge that it ever happened.

Why not, I'd asked. It was naive in retrospect. A stupid question that only a child could ask, and maybe that's why she entertained it. But, after all, she always entertained my questions.

Different reasons, she said. All sorts. No one in this family likes to acknowledge our past because it's too painful to remember. So instead they just pretend like nothing ever happened. What murder? What bullet? But the past is a thing that needs confronting, Baby, don't you ever forget that. You ignore it, hope it'll go away, let it push you around, and it'll haunt you for the rest of your days. You need to turn to it the first time it gives you shit, puff that little chest out as far as it'll reach, and show it who's boss. You understand me?

No, Mom, I sure don't. But one day I will.

Does Clover know? I asked.

No, Mom said. Just you. It's our secret now.

But as shocking as it was to my adolescent ears, Angela's story was missing something. It had no voice of its own. No breath. No blood running through its veins. An endless series of living moments—days, night, holidays—an entire life led. All of it reduced to a sentence. All of them reduced to their archetypical best: the innocent woman, the orphaned children, the evil husband. It was in moments like that—tales told of people long dead—that family becomes history, relatives reduced to mere characters, the totality of all that they were gone forever, lost to genealogy, imparted to me through streaming tears.

So there it was—our origin story.

I guess you could say that although The Sick Parents Club was officially formed in 1996, in a little patch of dirt in Queens, New York, it really began decades before any of my friends were even born. July 22nd, 1939, to be precise.

The shot rang out early that morning, to a household of children who didn't yet know that they were halfway to being orphans. The four children—my great aunts and uncles—had gone to sleep normal, and with the squeeze of a trigger they'd awoken forever deformed. That bullet ricocheted, as bullets do, hitting every single one of them, and lodging itself deep inside. So deep, in fact, that not a single one realized they'd been hit until years after it happened.

There were no survivors that day, even though there were many.

The club that would be named years later was formed when that bullet pierced the back of my great grandmother's skull. Her oldest daughter, my grandmother, was our first club member. And, eventually, through the damage done to her that day, she'd end up sponsoring my mom.

Why did we call it a club? Because a club is a collection of people who share something in common. In that, it doesn't need to be spoken into existence like some magic spell. It was always there, insomuch as the people who comprised the club were always there, sharing experiences through generations that held them together, despite all of their other differences.

How fragile a thing a family is, that one man with a single bullet can ruin everything! Who created that thing more magical than the one that danced its murderous way through JFK's motorcade in '63? Maybe it was born in the Old World, where the crimes of family were buried in an unmarked grave; forged in the unknowable misery of generations, and kept in a special box until such a time as its evil was required. When it finally crossed the Atlantic, to one day be loaded in my great grandfather's gun, it carried with it the promise of all dark secrets kept—to destroy; to end; to bathe the potential of the New World in oblivion.

Then, into the chamber of a fool being commanded by a diseased brain it went, to do its duty at a time of its master's choosing. That time, as history would have it, was the morning of July 22nd, 1939.

The day that will live on in familial infamy.

The day my great grandfather slaughtered his wife in cold blood.

The day my club was formed.

THE BASTARD KING

While this story is in no way lacking in bad men, ranging from the generally stupid to the outright villainous, they must all bow down to the one who started my family down the long and winding road we now find ourselves revisiting—the King of All Bastards, ladies and gentlemen, entering stage right. . .

His name was Thomas—that's the bullshit American translation—dude's real name was Athanasios, and he was, as his name would imply, one of a wave of immigrants who flooded these shores looking for a better life at the turn of the twentieth century. As it turned out, America did, in fact, hold a better life than the one he'd known back in Kalamata.

But the American Dream could be a fickle little bitch, as Thomas was soon to find out.

Not much is known (nothing, really) about his earlier life in Greece, save that he was an ambitious and handsome young man who, like every handsome young man, wanted to marry a beautiful girl and start a life. As fate would have it, that girl was my great grandmother and future murder victim, Angelikh.

She was from an affluent Greek family, and Thomas' plebeian roots simply weren't going to fly with the parents. The man had to do better, and where else to make one's fame and fortune? America, stupid, where else was there ever?

Then, in Godfather II—like fashion, my great grandfather came to the shores of New York in search of fortune. As it turns out, he found it. Like everything else, the details are sketchy, but he made his money in an olive oil business he started with some partners, and before long he returned to Kalamata and married Angela.

Oh, wait! I skipped the most important part of our otherwise cliche immigrant story.

Somewhere between A and B, our boy (who was apparently known for his love of all women of the night), contracted Syphilis, unbeknownst to anyone. This fact would come to make all the difference in the course of my family's history, because by the time 1939 rolled around (and from all accounts, probably way before that), Thomas was good and insane. Murderously insane. Proper crazy.

These are the moments I have to do my absolute best to not judge. I'm supposed to just tell you the story, right? Be the objective narrator. Just the facts, ma'am. But my ability to not stop at this point in the story and fucking scream is limited. The thing about the murder is that it wasn't Thomas' first rodeo. He'd never killed anyone (that we know of), but he had tried to kill his wife going on ten times before he finally got the job done. Now, I have to wonder, how many times does your husband have to try to kill you before you start to reconsider your options?

Maybe that's hindsight bias. 20/20 and all that, right? Who am I to judge? Maybe nobody, but what I can say with all the certainty in the world is that if Angela had come to her damn senses maybe I wouldn't be writing these words today.

My grandmother wouldn't have finished her adolescence as the de facto mother of four other siblings. Maybe she wouldn't have married the scum of the earth (my grandfather). And maybe my grandfather wouldn't have abused my mom. You get the point, right? Standard Butterfly Effect logic.

So there he is, ladies and gentlemen, my great grandfather Thomas, the Bastard King. Now understand that I call him a bastard not as description of what a bad man he was, but because a bastard is a man with dubious origins; no longer pure, debased.

That was him—the man who sat firmly atop of the family tree I was falling from, hitting every branch on the way down.

FIRST GENERATION HEALTHY

Always two. Definitely four. Occasionally six and eight. Rarely ten. Never twelve.

More than ten and I would have agreed to treatment, despite the revulsion I would have experienced at being the latest in my family to count a therapist as one of my primary caregivers. See, I had OCD before it was cool. Before the whole world started using it in grammatically nonsensical ways— *"I'm sooo OCD!"*

When I was a kid, even numbers were the master, and I the slave; powerless to act against the forces of oppression that compelled me to open and close my kitchen cabinets the perfect number of times, or else! And what was that so-called perfect number? Well, it varied. There were no hard and fast rules when it came to childhood anxiety disorders, but there were some best practices—*always two. Definitely four. Occasionally six and eight. Rarely ten. Never twelve.*

Sometimes Mom would catch me compulsing.

"Baby, what are you doing?"

That's when I'd turned around, horrified because I'd been

shocked out of my make-believe world where even numbers made things better. "Oh, nothing. Just getting a bowl."

I did the same with books. If I was lying in bed reading at night, every time I turned a page I'd have to lift the book over my head exactly two times before I could read any more. I'm sure I looked properly insane, but my brain told me it was the right thing to do.

Clover and I mostly were spared the worst of the crazy, but we still got the consolation prizes of a minor case of obsessive-compulsive disorder, and extreme introversion, respectively. I guess, technically, introversion isn't a disorder, but sometimes it made her act strange enough that it was hard to tell the difference. In the lottery that was mental illness, Mom and Dad hit the Win for Life. Clover and I had to be content with our *711* five-dollar scratch off win.

With the genetics we were working with it was a small miracle that we came out as stable as we were. While our two fertilized eggs were busy replicating their way to making us human, Vegas odds put us coming out normal at about a +10,000. Could have made a Rockefeller-esque fortune putting some change on how fucked up we'd be one day.

Depression, anxiety and the occasional sprinkle of psychosis were woven into the family DNA, same as the chromosomes for brown hair and eyes. Happiness was surely there too, buried somewhere so deep inside of our double helix, waiting for the next Crick and Watson to discover it. But, despite what reads like an insurmountable genealogy, we were alright. I always tried to look at the bright side of things, so I didn't see Clover and I as third generation crazy, I saw us as first generation healthy.

Just like the children of immigrants, we were being raised by people whose life experiences were completely different than ours. Mom and Dad had decided that their homeland was just too fucked up to stay and raise a family—time to pack their shit and set sail for *The Land of Normal*—shirts on their backs, five dollars in their wallets—all those cliches. We owe them a debt for their sacrifice, even if (like actual immigrants) they brought some of their old-world issues on the boat with them (they could never get rid of them all, no matter how much they tried), and even if we sometimes got embarrassed when their accents sounded a little too thick, we still owed them our sanity. We owed them our untraumatized little lives.

But their way of seeing the world was one we'd never truly understand, and vice versa. But that was by design— their deign. Their sacrifice. Their willingness to draw a line in the ground and say no more. Even by the ages of thirty-whatever, they'd lived the collective lives of twenty people— filled with the kind of shit we could only hear stories about but never really understand. This left them with that old world sense of entitlement—the belief that they'd experienced the harsh realities of life (which, of course, filled them with a secret knowledge of how things 'really' were), whereas we were just some spoiled little kids who didn't know what it was like for your dad to creep into your room at night and touch you inappropriately, or to have your drunk father beat your ass after you'd managed to avoid such a fate all day from the gangs at school. We were 'Generation Pussy' to them. They never stopped to consider that the new world, our spoiled little piece of 1980's suburbia, was the way things were meant to be. Mom and Dad were a contradiction like that—aware enough to know that something had gone wrong at the very stage of life their own children were at now, yet fucked up enough to not realize that most people didn't go through that kind of shit. This was the framework of childhood where our story really begins, circa 1996.

While we admired and respected our parent's bravery, we were ignorant of their life experiences, and that ignorance served as an invisible generational line; a mental health chasm that could never quite be bridged by either side. Our parents had no real conception of what it looked like to be healthy. It was an abstraction, a far-off concept, a cognitive land of milk and honey.

Reality would prove far more complex.

THE CHILDREN OF SICK PARENTS

If you've never heard of The Meadows you're certainly not alone.

It wasn't famous. No celebrities ever lived there, and not a single president ever passed through.

But it was a place like no other, full of the same wonders and terrors that all neighborhoods hold when you spend your formative years in them. Understand that I use the past tense not because a nuclear warhead destroyed the place the day after I moved out, but because The Meadows that I'm going to describe was The Meadows of the 1990's. The geography remains, but the place I grew up in is long gone, replaced by The Meadows of now, a place full of people and experiences that I can't speak to with any degree of certainty.

My family, the Dunbars, were OG's—we'd lived there forever, and that living took place in either apartments or duplexes, depending on which street you lived on, and we were more than content with our smaller-than-house homes. It was Queens, so our streets had numbers, not names. Names were some House Kid shit. My block was 71st Crescent, which sat as one of the many cross streets to 88th Avenue.

Carmine lived a block away, and so did Damien and Serafina, eventually.

The Meadows was large geographically, but it was broken up into little regions made up of a series of blocks, and each of those had all the boxes of small-town suburban life checked off. Everyone knew everyone else's business—the good, the bad, and the mentally ill. Secrets were something that very few people had, especially if you had the kind of stories that made neighborhood headlines. For us, that meant everyone knew about that time Dad got taken away by the police for erratic behavior, or that Mom had to quit her job in the city because of a mental breakdown. Because our family antics were the topic of many a family dinner in the neighborhood, my sister and I got the brunt of it at school. The adults at least knew how to be discreet and keep the gossip within the confines of their own home. Their kids were a different story. They had no social filters, and weren't embarrassed to call us out.

At school we were the 'crazy kids', the ones with the 'psycho' mom and 'crackhead' dad. We heard it all, and we heard it often. Bullies seemed to have no gas tank when it came to their particular brand of cruelty. But like everything else in our lives, Clover and I reacted to the ridicule very differently. I externalized while she internalized. In other words, I got pissed at the assholes shouting at us, while Clover got mad at our parents for giving the bullies ammunition in the first place.

"Why can't our parents just be normal like everyone else's are?" she asked me one day in the sixth grade, after Julie James called our mom a psycho in gym class (and yes, that was the girl's real name, yet she thought we were the ones with the fucked up parents!).

"Who do you know who has normal parents?" I asked

64

right back. "Ours are just a little less normal than the other kids'. So what? It's not their fault."

"There you go again," she said, rolling her eyes like she was inclined to do when she thought I was defending our parents from what she perceived as their bad behavior. "Defending Mom and Dad."

"Isn't that what you're supposed to do?"

"What?"

"Defend your family? Isn't that kind of what family is for?"

"I'm not sure what family's for anymore, Nathan."

She was prone to dramatic shit like that—extreme statements that were a little too mature and negative for her age. But that was Clover, and despite her tendencies towards resenting our parents, I loved her as much as I loved anyone in this world, even though we disagreed often and aggressively on that topic. We weren't those typical cat and dog siblings. As brothers and sisters went, we actually got along really well, except when it came to stuff about our family. We had conversations like this all the time:

"You think Mom asked to be born to a crazy, screwed up mom and an abusive dad?"

"Obviously not, Nathan, who would ask for that? Come on."

"That's my point, Clover. Why do you think she is the way she is?"

"It's more complicated than that. You're trying to make it too simple."

"I'm not trying to make it anything, I'm just telling the truth. If anything, you're the one who's making it too simple."

"How?"

"Because you want to make it like Mom is bad, and it's

her fault kids at school make fun of us, but you know that's not true. It's not her fault. She's the one going through some real dark stuff, Clover, not us."

My sister rolled her eyes, but that's how I saw it. My mom was the ultimate victim of victims. It's like trauma was a family heirloom, something to be handled with the utmost care, never broken, and passed down with the utmost expediency and pride. The second my mom was old enough to form memories she was forming bad ones that would haunt her the rest of her life. Ones that would be laid out in lurid detail for a whole graduating class worth of psychologists.

Of course, she said weird stuff. Of course, she could barely function. Of course, she was just being the victim she was raised to be. But Clover always had trouble seeing that side. Easier to blame them for the kids at school being shitty to us and our friends.

School.

Never were there six worse letters put together in the entire English language. Seventh and eighth grade were one thing, but high school was a snake pit that rivaled the worst of Indiana Jones' nightmares, filled not just with those regular poisonous snakes, either. I'm talking about those rare Australian suckers who could kill you with nothing more than a sideways glance. No antidote yet discovered.

None of us were engineered to survive that environment, but the law demanded we spend the majority of our waking hours collecting some psychological trauma that would stay with us forever. So, like conscripts, we did our duty without complaint, working on our post traumatic stress management with each ringing of the morning bell. We were that poor cow in Jurassic Park being lowered into the Velociraptor cage as a sacrificial snack. That first bastard off the boat on D-Day.

High school was a completely different thing from all the

other years of school, even though we were essentially with the same kids we'd always known. Once we entered that big-ass building the whole social dynamic we'd known our whole lives shifted—and almost instantly. Kids formed tribes. The neighbor who had always played at our house and drank all of our orange soda suddenly got himself a heroine addiction and hair dyed jet black. The girl who Mom used to call 'sweet' in elementary because she was always smiling at dismissal and saying polite shit suddenly became the school whore, giving out blowjobs like mini Kit Kats on Halloween.

That building just changed everything. Everything except me and my friends. We were always the same. Year one was bewildering as all fuck, mostly because we were a stateless nation—a lowly collection of nerdy refugees who'd been taken from our homeland in a Diaspora with no end in sight. We all coped in different ways.

There was the aforementioned Carmine, my best friend since before forever, who attempted to ease his high school woes by going on some frenetic prowl to get with any girl he could. It rarely worked. There was the one time this girl Misty went over his house on that rare occasion his family wasn't home and made out with him, but she did that with just about everyone. It was bad luck that the first girl he encountered was one of the wave of sluts, because it gave him the false impression that all girls were like that. He really thought that he didn't have to do anything but walk up and say hello, and then poof—he'd have his tongue down their throats. Kid found out the hard way.

Still, he did better than me. When it came to girls, my luck was on par with that degenerate who always hung out at the corner store, spending his last five dollars on a Quick Pick lottery ticket—I played too often and never won. But I was fooled by the older kids in the neighborhood. They all seemed to be hanging out with girls—like Carmine's brothers and some of the other guys, there were always girls with them. So somewhere along the line I became deluded into thinking that girls just came standard with the growing up package, along with acne and crippling insecurity.

My sister went full throttle introvert when we started high school—to the point where her science teacher actually recommended that she speak with the school psychologist to make sure she didn't have some kind of selective mutism. She's just strange, I told her teacher, nothing clinical. Clover wasn't actually strange when you knew her—or when she knew you—but her default mode wasn't to talk to people, and when she was socially uncomfortable she went full blank stare mute on you. I think it was three weeks before she actually spoke in school.

"What's wrong with you?" I'd ask. We shared a 6th period lunch. "Why are you being weird?"

"Introvert problems," she'd say. "You wouldn't understand."

"Try me," I'd tell her. "But that means you'll actually have to say words."

"I'm not scared to say words, you know that as well as anyone. I just don't know what to say sometimes. Like, most times. I'm in my own head a lot, that's all."

"I'm in my own head also, but they're not sending me to the school shrink for being weird. That's some next level stuff."

"I just told the psychologist I was an extreme introvert, and that my teacher was overreacting. She understood."

"Wow," I joked. "So you actually spoke to an adult you don't know, AND told them something personal. You're making strides, kid. Pretty soon your teachers won't think you have a clinical disorder."

"Don't joke about that, Nathan."

"What? Having a disorder? Why not?" She shot me the look—the one that conferred 'you know damn well why not' without a word being spoken. She could be humorless when it came to Mom and Dad.

The only person who pulled her out of her head at school —or in general—was Carmine. She had a secret crush on him since before I could remember. Nothing ever happened between them in high school, mostly 'cause Clover was too shy and Carmine was too oblivious, but I used to give her shit whenever I had the chance, like brothers are supposed to do.

My friends and I were losers, but don't take that the wrong way. The difference between being a loser and being a victim may seem unimportant—a trivial and crude semantic distinction that only a teenaged boy would conceive. Maybe so. But where I come from, subtle distinctions were everything.

In terms of life experience, a victim was that stereotypical kid who got shoved in a locker and bullied with no care as to who was watching. A loser was the kid everyone made fun of in private, who didn't have too many friends, but that didn't get messed with enough to screw his or her head up. I was that kid. The one who hated school because he got shit on a daily basis, but who never internalized any of it as being true. The way I saw things, people could talk all the shit they wanted, as long as I couldn't hear it. Hell, even if I could, I wasn't apt to do much about it, but if you'd laid hands on me or, even worse, messed with someone I loved, you'd catch these hands.

I was complex—not some one-dimensional character with a pocket protector, thick glasses, and some inborn passivity that demanded I accept other people's shit without opposition. I wasn't a victim, even though I was raised by them.

Despite my fundamental nerdiness, I had that braggadocios swag that was rare in someone with my personality; a thing inside of me that compelled me to show the world what I could do if it gave me half a chance to do so. My best friends Carmine and Damien saw this side of me on the basketball court.

"And one!" I'd yell after shooting right over Damien's pathetic attempt at defense.

"Stop bragging. I hate playing you."

"You hate playing me 'cause I whoop your ass. The bragging is just extra."

"You're just extra."

"Good one." My sarcasm was a wild animal whose spirit could never be broken. Attempts at domestication were doomed to fail.

"Shut up. Let's just play."

"Don't be all sensitive. We can play loser gets ball, instead of winner." We had to play like this all time. We didn't do teams outside of two-on-two. Maybe three-on-three if some outsiders showed up, but outsiders rarely showed up. The court was ours—part of the geography that made up what we just called The Back, which was a communal backyard for those of us—which was all of us—who didn't have real backyards of our own like those kids at school who grew up in houses. Those House Kids lived a few blocks away, and they might as well have been a different species—the last roaming Neanderthals of our hood. We saw them occasionally, mostly from a distance across 88th Avenue, a street that divided us in more ways than one. The separation of our geographies wasn't much in terms of actual feet, but 88th might as well have been a border between neighboring countries.

"I don't need special rules. Keep your pity." Damien was

sensitive like that. Prone to outbursts when he was losing, which was always. Kid couldn't shoot a basketball to save his life, and when he tried it looked something like if an Olympic Javelin throw and a proper basketball shot had a premature baby.

"I'm just saying, it might help you out. If we play losers at least it's fair."

"It's fair now, asshole!" Damien was delusional when it came to his skill set, but he was our friend, and we loved the kid even though we gave him enough shit to last a lifetime.

Even when I puffed my chest out, like I did whenever Damien dared to challenge me to a game, I never felt that I was better than anyone else, but I could sure do some things better, and I wanted everyone to see. It cut both ways. I was fascinated by people who had the skills I lacked. Kids who were good at math were like fucking magicians to me. I could have watched them move numbers around a white board all day like watching David Blaine do some crazy illusionist shit on TV. And, given my moment, I liked to shine too.

Where did that come from? See, before my parents lost their collective minds—in different ways, for different reasons—they did, in fact, grant me and my sister Clover the Sleeping Beauty-like gift of a thing that protected us from a lot of things that could have hurt us. That gift was self confidence, self esteem, a sense of who we were as human beings. That may sound like nothing, but it was everything. It was the difference between believing what the other kids say about you and having an invisible force field surrounding you at all times, off of which their cruelty could bounce and fall to the ground. We valued ourselves when no one else could, and that alone protected us.

But being a loser wasn't just about being rejected. It had a culture all its own, and I was a nerd, through and through, as most losers are. To lay claim to that title, I had to make the following concessions:

1.) I was cool being alone in my room with a stack of comics, for any length of time. As long as I had Jean Grey and Wolverine, I'd never be lonely.

2.) I was petrified of talking to girls, especially Serafina.

3.) Not counting my sister, I had exactly three friends, and three friends only.

Why did I have so few friends? Because when you're a loser you don't always have a tribe, you don't always have a people. You're a stateless nation, wandering the Earth in search of a homeland. But I was lucky. I found mine when I was a kid. Our homeland was The Back. Our people were my friends. And our tribe? Serafina gave that a name, one night in my room after she came over to listen to some music and bullshit a little.

"We're losers," I told her. "But we're losers together. So, like, a collection of losers, I guess."

"There's something else that we have in common you know? I was thinking about the other day, after my dad finished yelling at me that the house was dirty. You know, right before he dropped a pizza box on the floor for me to clean up and passed out from drinking too much."

"Jesus, I'm sorry. I kind of got that vibe from him."

"Not a vibe," she said. "That's him. That's who he's always been, but it's gotten really bad since Mom died." She stopped for a second, lost in thought, lost in memory, then came back like she was woken from a dream. "Sorry, you don't want to hear about my problems, you have plenty of your own. What's the deal with your mom?"

Anyone else who asked that question in that way would have gotten a smack from me, but I knew she didn't mean it like it sounded. Plus, it was impossible to ignore that something was off with Mom. She tried to put on her brave face when people came over, but mostly she stayed in her room. The few times she ventured out she was never dressed, even if it was the middle of the afternoon.

"Depression," I confessed. "Do you know what that is?"

"Like being really really sad?"

"Kind of, but it's worse than that. Sadness goes away eventually."

"And Depression doesn't?"

"For some people I guess. I'm not sure, I don't really know anyone else who's depressed. But for Mom it never really seems to go away. I guess if sadness is like a cold that you get better from in a week, Depression is like. . . like missing a leg. It's always there, probably something you're born with, or something that happens causes it, but it never grows back. You just have to learn to live with it."

"You talk like a book, did anyone ever tell you that?"

I laugh. "Clover tells me that all the time. She does the same thing."

"You're right. Maybe you two will be writers one day."

"Fat chance. I hate English."

"Well who doesn't? Mr. Brad is a dick."

"Super dick. I hate him. We all hate him. I think he came to school drunk the other day."

"Oh, he definitely did."

We both laughed hysterically, and it felt like a needed break from what we were just discussing. She leaned over to pick up my headphones again, but I stopped her.

"Clover thinks that Mom's crazy. Both my parents, actually, just like those kids at school say."

I don't know why I blurted that confession out. It was bothering me. It always bothered me, and for some reason in

Serafina's presence honesty flowed out of me. She listened, furrowing her brow like she didn't like what she was hearing. "And what do you think?"

I took a deep breath. "I think they've acted crazy enough times for her to think that and not be wrong, but I don't like the word crazy. It makes it seem like they're just lunatics. They're not lunatics."

"Do you know where that word comes from?"

"Which word?"

"Lunatics. You just used it twice. Do you know where it comes from?" I nod my head. "The moon. They used to think that people with mental illness were affected by the moon, so they called them lunatics, after the word lunar. Where do you think the whole Werewolf myth comes from?"

"So back in the day they thought being mentally ill was like being a werewolf or something?"

She laughed. "Something like that. I don't think your parents are crazy. We all have issues, right? Some just have way more than others."

"You too?"

She laughed, but it wasn't a laugh like something was funny, it was the kind of laugh you let out when someone says something particularly stupid. "Yeah, Nathan. Me especially. Have you met my father?"

"I've met him a few times, yeah. Mostly the times Carmine and I call on your brother to play ball."

"He's. . . different since our mom died. Like, really different. I love you guys, but moving here was a little traumatic. Everything's different."

"I understand," I said, even though I had no idea what it was like to move. We'd moved once, when Clover and I were two, from the apartments surrounding the Oak Grove to here, less than five minutes away, but I had no idea what it was like to upend my entire life and move to a new place with new friends. "It must be hard. And the assholes at school don't help, do they?"

"No," she said somberly. "They do the opposite of helping. Whatever the right word for that is."

"Don't worry about the right word," I told her. "I understand what you mean."

"You ever think that's why all of us are such good friends?"

"Why's that?"

"We're all kind of. . . what's the word?"

"Losers," I finished for her. That's what we were. Not really, but that's how the rest of the kids our age saw us. Sometimes I even think that's how our parents saw us. We were a collection of rejects who spent time together, as rejects tend to do. Damien was a walking target. Clover was so introverted people thought she was weird and rude. Carmine and I were too into comics and other nerdy stuff for our own good, and Serafina was a free spirit who dressed weird, dyed her hair, and listened to strange music that no one knew. It wasn't just Damien, we were all moving targets. "But finish your thought. You said that we all had something in common besides just being losers."

"It was about our families. All of them, from what I can tell."

"What do you mean?"

"Don't you realize, Nate? We're all the children of sick parents."

Our name was born that night, of a hushed declaration of things I didn't fully understand at the time, and of a shared bond so obvious that I hardly realized its existence.

THE FIERY ONE

The things that alter the course of our lives don't always announce themselves. Sometimes, like a pop quiz in science that'll make you sweat in places you didn't know existed, those life altering moments just appear in front of you, ready-or-not. My ready-or-not moment happened when the Gilmores moved into the Meadows.

They moved in a few years before everything happened, right after we'd just finished our last elementary school rotation. A few months later we'd be moving onto the unexplored frontier of middle school (more on that drama later in the story). We were all scared shitless about it, but our anxiety took a backseat to the endless possibilities of summer, which included the excitement of a new family moving in.

It was the first day of July. The fourth was one of my family's favorite days of the year—one of those rare days where the shadow of mental illness wasn't cast over every little thing, we could just have fun and be a family together. My dad always stockpiled fireworks that he got from a hookup he had in Chinatown, and that year we had enough explosives in our house to invade a small South American country.

But before we lit enough bottle rockets, M-80's, and Roman Candles to light the night sky, the Gilmores made their entry into our lives. It was a year before Mom's depression got really bad, which meant that she still left the house from time to time, and was capable of normal human interaction. It was a big deal when they moved in, because not too many families had in a long time. Clover was excited because she always complained about the complete lack of girls her age in the neighborhood. "Do you think they have a daughter? Like, one my age?"

"No idea," I told her. "Who cares?"

"I care, asshole. You wouldn't understand."

"What?"

"You've got a million boys around. There are no girls."

"What are you talking about? There's whats-his-face's sister. The one a few blocks over."

"Merle?"

"Yeah! Merle, that's it. Why don't you ever hang with her if you're so desperate for female companionship?"

"Nathan, Merle is nineteen, and everyone says she's a heroine addict."

"Oh. I never heard that part."

"Which? Her age or her drug habit."

"Either, actually. She looks young."

"She is young, dummy. Just not young like we are. I'm not sure Mom and Dad would be cool with me making friends with a college-aged druggie. Last thing this family needs is another issue."

On move in day Mom and Dad made the Gilmores a casserole and some sugar cookies like it was the 1950's (those habits died hard) and forced us to walk it over to them in our finest clothes. This is stupid, we told Mom. No one does this anymore, this is just how you were raised. We'll just see the kids when they come outside and say hi. We don't need all this formality.

Shut up and get dressed, she told me, we're going. So we did. The Dunbars took their neighborly food and marched in formation a block down until we were at their front door. I was given the job (I'm still not sure why) of ringing their bell, and about five seconds after I did I got to lay my teenaged eyes on the most beautiful girl I'd ever seen in my life.

"Hi," said the most beautiful girl in the world. "Can I help you?"

Mom stepped in and did her Mom thing. We're the Dunbars, she explained, are your parents home? My Dad is, the girl replied. Hold on. We stood there, casserole in hand (Clover held that, it was my job to guard the sugar cookies), waiting to meet the patriarch of the new family that just moved in. That's when he stepped forward, looking a hot mess.

"Hello," the short man said. He smelled of cigarettes.

"Pleased to meet you," Dad said, his hand already extended and a weird fake smile on his face. "We're the Dunbars. We live down the block. Just wanted to welcome you to the neighborhood."

I remember him looking like he had no idea what this kind of ceremony was all about. We all did our introductions, and that's when I handed the cookies over like we were exchanging hostages. "Here," I said, extending the tin to Mr. Gilmore.

He took it from me with that same baffled expression on his face. I wasn't one for formality, but I did know the dance, so it struck me as strange, even as a kid, that he didn't seem to want to invite us in, or even open the door more than the mandatory crack that was required to put his body in between. "Thank you," he said, taking the tin from me and holding it in midair like he wasn't sure quite what to do.

As I would come to know very soon, Mr. Gilmore had issues—a lot of them—and it didn't take a Ph.D. in Psychology to see that. We all stood there on his stoop in this awkward silence, my parents expecting the only other adult to at least be civil—maybe say a little something about himself, introduce his family, or even invite us in, but none of that happened. The girl was still standing outside, and she took over. It seemed like a role she was used to.

"Thank you so much for the food, Mrs. Dunbar."

"Beth," Mom corrected. "You can call me Beth, sweetheart. And you're very polite. . ."

"Serafina," she said, extending her hand to shake Mom's. "I'm sorry I didn't say my name, did I? This is my dad, Henry."

"Hank is fine," he interrupted.

"And my brother, Damien, just ran to the store to grab a few things. I'm sure he'll be back in a few minutes. Would you like. . ."

"Thanks again. We'll see you guys around I'm sure." Hank cut off what I expected to be an invitation into their duplex, and the way he did it made me question him immediately. He clearly didn't want us inside, but I didn't know why. Dad read the situation and we said our goodbyes.

Once we were far enough away I spoke my mind. "That guy was rude as hell."

"He's probably overwhelmed with the move." Dad was the king of excuses.

"I guess, but still."

"Not everyone is as well mannered as you," Mom said, smiling and putting a hand on my shoulder. "Give him time,

I'm sure he'll warm up. The girl was very nice. She had a strange name, what was it?"

"Serafina," Clover answered, the happiness in her voice palpable. "I don't know anyone else at school who has that name."

"I'm sure you'll be best friends," I joked. "You and your new friend with the weird name."

"Shut up!"

When we got back I remember thinking how father and daughter didn't match. He was rude, looked a mess, smelled like shit, and was the kind of guy you tell little kids to avoid on Halloween because he'll chase you away. But Serafina was the opposite—she was well dressed, her hair was perfect, and she seemed like the adult in the situation.

"Where was their mom?" I asked.

"Don't know. Maybe she was out with the boy getting groceries or something."

I'll save you the suspense. She wasn't out with *the boy*, whose name was Damien by the way (heretofore referred to as 'colorblind' by Carmine and I because of the crazy way he dressed), their mom had died of Cancer. Hank had moved here for a fresh start, and as soon as I learned this a lot of that first encounter seemed to make sense. He needed a wife— needed a woman to tell him to shave and stop drinking so much and clean up whatever it was that was causing the stench to emanate from their place. But she was dead, and now Serafina seemed to be the woman of the house.

About a week later, brother and sister emerged from that cave when they saw us all hanging out in the back, doing our usual summer thing. There was a little park in the back where we all chilled when the weather was nice, in between video games, endless basketball, and generally wandering around trying to keep ourselves busy. Me, Clover and Carmine were a tight unit, but we were more than open to adding to the tribe. We were actually excited at the prospect of new friends, especially going into a new school the next year. None of us were very popular (which is a polite way of saying we were fucking social rejects), so having more of a tribe just seemed like good economics. But we didn't know the Gilmore kids yet.

When they finally emerged, they were cool as hell—Serafina in particular. Damien was a little south of cool, but he was a good kid, and we all got along right away. When Serafina came out in a Clash vintage tee I think I fell in some kind of love. "You like punk?" I asked.

"Of course I do. You don't?"

It was the perfect answer, and despite what I knew would be Clover's intense jealousy, I knew that I'd just made one of the greatest friends I'd ever have.

No Fate But What We Choose

Some people are just cool.

We can define that concept in different ways, but I think you know what I mean. I'm not talking number of friends in school, or that certain aura some people just have. When I say that Serafina was cool I mean that she was one of those handful of girls who come into your life that skirt the line between friendship and love. They're always free spirits, and always flirty enough that you can't tell if that's just who they are, or if they like you like that. You don't ask, because that would be weird, so you mostly spend your time around them confused as hell as to what your own intentions should be, but you cherish every moment because they're easy to talk to, they like what you like, and they make you laugh like no one else in the world. Some of those girls you try to date, some you don't. I didn't know what Serafina was to me in those terms, but I did know that in the short time I knew her she'd become one of my favorite people on the planet.

For starters, she was into the same movies and music that I was. We used to talk about things like what kind of tattoos we were gonna get when we were older, and which position we'd play if we ever started our own band.

"Lead guitar," she'd say. "There's no other role. Lead is everything."

"Yeah, if you're in Led Zeppelin. If you wanna form a punk band all you need is three chords, some crazy energy, and dyed hair doesn't hurt."

"Dyed hair never hurts." That week her own dyed hair was a light shade of orange, mixed with some of her natural blonde, and a single streak of green, that ran down the back of her head. We were into the same kind of music, bonding over favorite punk rock records. Even so, sometimes she made ridiculous arguments. "Green Day is not a punk band," she'd proclaim, like she was an expert in all things three-chord related.

"Don't say crazy shit just to say it."

"When do I ever do that?" she'd ask, knowing full well that the answer was 'right now.'

"Right now!" I helped move her inner dialogue along. "By what crazy ass criteria are you making that claim?"

"On the fact that you can sing along to their songs. If you can sign along it's not punk."

"Two words," I said defiantly. "The. Ramones."

"Overrated."

"You're insane," I'd tell her.

"You wouldn't be the first to have that opinion of me."

"You're crazy about the Ramones. They're melodic as hell, and just about every punk band will say they're an influence."

"Okay, fine, I'll give you the Ramones, but that doesn't change my stance on Green Day. Not a punk band."

"I feel like it's become a cool thing to hate on them just because they made it. It's not their fault that everyone loves *Dookie*."

She snickered. "Did you just hear yourself?"

I replayed my last line in my head and couldn't help but smile. "Did not hear it as I said it, but now that you pointed it out."

We started laughing, so loudly that everyone in the cafeteria looked at us like the freaks we were.

Our friendship was an offshoot of her best-friendship with my sister, Clover. The two of them were peas and carrots, always spending time together, always sharing secrets the rest of the world wasn't privy to. But we had our own thing that revolved around our respective nerdiness, and there was plenty of that to go around. Bands, comics, TV shows, movies, she could hang in any topic of conversation I'd bring up.

Serafina was a girlfriend without actually being one. She was someone who I was instantaneously close with—the girl I told things that I never told anyone else. When the sadness of home became too much, I'd ask her to take walks with me, and our walks were epic! No strolls around the block for us, no sir. That girl could W-A-L-K, and as our teenaged legs took us places neither of us had been before outside of the passenger seat of a car, we shared things with each other that were for our ears only.

On the first walk we ever took, I told her about my even number thing. She never treated weirdness like there was anything wrong with it. Consider the power in that for a second—imagine telling some beautiful, mysterious girl who just moved in a few houses down from you that you needed to count things in even numbers because you believed (like, really really believed) that terrible shit would be bestowed upon you and yours if you didn't. No one would do that, right? Most girls would run for the fucking hills, and tell all of their friends what a nut you were along the way. But Serafina wasn't most girls. She always just seemed fascinated by whatever I told her. No judgement, no raised eyebrows, no uncomfortable moments between us. In fact, she engaged in the ultimate gesture of understanding—she asked all sorts of questions.

"Why even numbers?"

"I don't know—just kind of how my brain works, I guess."

"Interesting. Like, how do you think your life would be different if you had to do things in odd numbers instead? Do you think you'd view the world totally differently?"

Shit like that. She asked questions that made me think about my own OCD like I was studying someone else besides myself. For the rest of that day I thought about the odd number question. I still don't have an answer to that one.

She never talked about her family much, and I never asked. Don't get me wrong, it wasn't that I wasn't interested, or that I wouldn't have lent her all of my ears for as long as she needed to tell me about whatever, it just never came up. She always asked about me, and I took for granted how intoxicating it can be to have that kind of focused attention from another person—especially one as beautiful as Serafina. Her eyes were piercing. They'd look into you as easily as they'd look at you, and there was a kind of trance they could put you in—a hypnotic state of wonderfulness from which you never ever wanted to wake. In that state I would have confessed to the Kennedy assassination, but she never manipulated me like that. If anything, she helped me understand my world much more clearly.

I once asked her a question that I've never asked anyone else—an inquiry that originated in the deepest recesses of my consciousness—a question that kept me awake at night. I never asked anyone about it, or even spoke the words aloud until she asked me what I was thinking one day after we stopped to rest on a park bench during one of our walks.

"Do you think that things can live in our DNA from a long time ago? Things that make us who we are."

"Well yeah," she said. "Isn't that kind of what DNA is?"

"No. . . I mean, yes, but that's not what I meant. You asked what I was thinking, right?"

"Uh-huh. I want to know what's going on in that brain of yours."

"Forget DNA. Do you think that who we come from—the family that we're from, makes us who we are? Even the people who lived before we lived. The ones who are so far up the family tree there wasn't even photography yet to record their faces. Do you think that those people somehow pass things along to later generations in their family?" She looked at me like she usually did—inquisitively—like I'd just asked her the most interesting thing she'd ever been asked.

"I think that they have to impact us, somehow, for good or for bad, but I couldn't tell you how that works. It's like a ripple effect. Who they were influenced their kids, and their kids influenced their kids, all the way until the family line gets to us and our parents. It's like a game of telephone."

"God, I hope that's not true." I didn't mean for that to come out that way, I really didn't. She looked at me, puzzled for the first time, and I felt bad about what I'd just said. "I hope it's not true because I come from bad men, Fina. Like, really bad. I hope that none of them live inside of me."

"What did the men do that was so bad?"

Not too many questions before or after that carried as much weight as that. I didn't know how to answer.

"I could make you a list. Bad guys doing bad shit. You name it. I come from 'The Men Who Hurt'."

"The who?" she asked, puzzled at my casual use of a phrase no one knew but me.

"I'm sorry, that was random. It's a name I came up with a while ago to describe the guys who hurt women. I don't know where it came from, just popped into my head one day, like a lot of things do."

"I like the name," she confessed. "But I want to know more."

"It's actually a thing I wrote. Like an essay, I guess, or just a bunch of paragraphs, if that has a name."

"You write?"

"I write. My mom was a writer. At least she wanted to be.'"

"But she wasn't?"

"No," I told her. "Not like she wanted to be. A lot of things didn't turn out the way she wanted them to. But I guess that happens to everyone."

"Maybe. Then again, maybe not. Who knows? But tell me the rest."

"What do you mean?"

"Your writing. Do you remember any of it, by heart?"

I started to panic. Telling someone that you wrote was one thing, but letting them see your actual work was something else. The idea of opening myself up like that—of being vulnerable—was really frightening. But I got lost in her eyes and told her the truth.

"I know that one—*The Men Who Hurt*. It's short. I wrote

it one night when I couldn't sleep because I was thinking about this."

"Tell it to me."

"It's short. Really short."

"I don't care how long it is—I just want to hear it. Tell me."

And I did. Out loud, like she asked me to.

The men who hurt look like the men who don't. They're legion; too numerous to count. I come from them. It's hard to tell which tribe has the numbers—the hurters or the normal men—and it would only be speculation anyhow. The bad ones blend like the chameleons I used to read about in Highlights magazine when I was a kid. They seem to be everywhere— at the store, behind you in line at Dunkin Donuts, at school, hell, they might even live inside your home. The first 'Hurter' that I ever knew was my father—and the woman my sister and I call Mom was neither his first nor his last victim—she was just the one who mattered most to me; the one whose pain shaped me into a man who won't ever hurt women the way he did—never.

When I was finished I felt as though I had no weight—my mind was racing and my spirit felt free. I don't know if it was just saying the words out loud, or having someone there who wanted to hear them.

"I loved that. It was darkly beautiful."

"Thank you," I said. It was surreal for someone to even know about my writing, let alone hear it spoken and compliment me for it. "You're the first—and probably only— person to hear that, or anything else I've written."

"You've written other things, too?"

"Oh yeah. Lots. Stories, essays. All kinds of things."

"I love that. Maybe you'll write about me one day," she said. I smiled, not knowing how profound her words were until decades later. "Listen, I don't want you to have to talk about anything you don't want to, but can I ask you something personal?"

"You already know more about me than most of my friends, so ask away."

"Why would you think that you're like any of. . . what did you call them? The hurters? You're not a bad person, Nathan. Why would you ever worry about something like that?"

It was a good question, and I'd never really had anyone question my own beliefs on this matter, mostly because I never shared my thoughts with anyone. If I'd asked Mom it just would have upset her. Dad was one of the guys I wrote about—at least he used to be, but it still counted in my teenaged mind. And Clover. . . Clover didn't want to discuss anything family related. So I shared my thoughts with the large yellow legal pads that my parents always kept in the wooden table in the living room. That's where my worries lived, where my fictional characters made their home, where all the imaginings that were only mine could come to life. But now, Serafina.

"I don't know," I told her. "How can I be descended from so many bad people, but not be one myself?"

"Maybe they're not bad people, Nathan. Maybe they just did bad things."

Bad things, I thought, like murdering their wives in the kitchen; like abusing their little girl. I was too entranced with Serafina to argue with her, but I couldn't accept that part of what she was saying, even if it was to comfort me.

"I don't think so," I told her. "There has to be a difference between bad people and good people who just do some bad things, but the things the men in my family have done cross that line to me. For fuck's sake, Fina, I share genetic material with murderers and abusers."

Again, no reaction. No shock. No wide-eyed horror. Just an open mind and ears, and a processing of what I'd just said. "So does every relative of every murderer and abusive person in history, Nathan. Probably millions of people at this point. Does that mean they all turned into their relatives? Of course not. You're not one of those men—you just hang out on the same family tree. I mean, do I seem anything like my brother or father to you?"

She really didn't. From the moment we met on her stoop that day they moved in, I always thought that she must have been adopted or something. Damien was my boy and Hank was, well, he was Hank, but Serafina seemed like she came from somewhere else—the adopted daughter of some other tribe who got lost one day and adopted by the Gilmores.

"No, you don't. No offense."

"None taken, silly, I brought it up. I know I'm not like them, and I'm okay with that. But my point isn't to talk about my family, it's to show you that one has nothing to do with the other—sometimes we can be just like our parents, and other times we can be nothing like them. It depends. It can go either way. And you're forgetting something."

"What?" I asked.

"That there are good men in your family. And bad women. And everything in between. Shades of grey, you know? You're just focusing on the one group because you know about them, but there are others, Nathan. There are always others."

A breeze came by. Sometimes the weather seemed like it was your own personal tool—like Storm in the X-men. It would thunderstorm when you got upset, a bright ray of sunshine might appear when you were happy. And in that instance, there was a gust of wind strong enough to feel yet gentle enough to blow Serafina's multicolored hair to the side in a way that made her seem angelic.

"I guess you're right," I answered. "I just always wonder where they all come from."

"Where do any of us come from?" she asked to the passing breeze. "Some things are taught to us, and others are inside of us always. It's just a matter of how those puzzle pieces get put together. And remember something else, okay? I want you to think about what I'm going to say whenever you're up late at night and you can't call me. Promise?"

"I promise. What is it?"

And then she put her hand on my arm, and I felt a jolt of electricity because I wasn't expecting it. "Even if you come from bad men, you can be the first good one. You can be the person who breaks that cycle. No fate but what we choose, Nathan. Be a good man like you're meant to be and forget the past."

We walked home after that, talking about lighter things and just being kids—just being new friends. Sometimes you don't appreciate things as they're happening. Only the passage of time let's you understand the impact of words or the profundity of moments that passed by in real time without notice. I don't remember what I had for dinner that night; couldn't tell you what I was assigned for homework. I don't recall if Mom was having a good day or a bad one, or if I talked to Carmine after I got home. All I remembered were her words.

No fate but what what we choose. . .

WHERE SERAFINA (AS ALL GIRLS INEVITABLY MUST) DATES THE WRONG GUY

I didn't know the word empath when I was in high school, but Serafina was as close to being one as you could get. She could be really sensitive—empathetic to a fault, and even when people were cruel to her she tried to understand what made them act that way. She was so forgiving that she didn't see what was painfully obvious to someone like me.

Enter Russell.

Stories don't have to have heroes in order to have villains. Sometimes the villains just exist on their own, perfectly unchallenged to rule their wicked kingdoms with impunity. In most stories good and evil come as a pair, but in real life the villains can come a la carte.

Like a lot of girls that I knew (including more than one in my family), Serafina had that recessive gene that made her predisposed to liking the wrong guys. A lot of women had it, lying dormant, waiting for the perfect social context for it to expose itself. In her case it was exposure to the giant database of good-looking douche bags that all high schools were populate with. And Serafina didn't just go for the wrong guys, she went for the bad guys.

When my sister told me that Serafina was going out on a date with Russell, I fucking screamed. That's no exaggeration. I lost all control of whatever part of the brain stops you from screaming like a lunatic when everything inside is telling you to scream like a lunatic. My parents rushed into my room in a panic because they thought, rationally, that I was being murdered by a pack of wolves. When they realized that I wasn't, that my guttural yelling was some teenaged drama, they went about their business, leaving my sister to calm me down, even though that wasn't happening.

"She's doing what?"

"I know. I tried to tell her."

"And?" I was still yelling. "How the hell could you let her go out with that fucker?"

"Let her? I'm not her mom. Shit, sorry, I shouldn't have said mom. I'm not. . . you know what I mean!"

"I know that she shouldn't be going out with Russel. No girl should."

"I warned her about him, for what it's worth."

Russell was a literary technique—the evil force necessary to balance out the good in any story worth telling, only he was a real person. A living, breathing, predating person. He was a hunter, and younger girls were his prey. A senior by the time my friends and I walked into Thomas Jefferson High, he was already infamous for his exploits with the opposite I sex. I guess all of the girls in his own grade knew better than to give him the time of day—or maybe too many of them had given him much more than just the time of day, and wanted to save the underclassmen from him. Whatever the history was, Russell went after girls who were younger and less experienced than him. They called him the V-card stealer because of his proclivity to fool freshman and sophomores into giving it up on the first or second date.

"Wait, what's a V-card?" I asked Carmine when we first heard the legend of old Russell.

"Are you stupid?"

"I'm not. I just don't know the lingo."

"It means virginity, dummy. As in, he takes it from as many girls as he can. Rumor has it that he and Jared have a running talley. Last I heard it was 4-5 in Jared's favor."

"How do you know all this? And why haven't I heard about the v-card thing?"

"I don't know about the second, but I heard from Allen."

"That kid has all the dirt."

"I know. It's his brother. He's in Russell's grade so he tells Allen everything."

Almost as if it were scripted, Jared and Russell walked by. They always had these smug smiles on their faces, as if they were the alphas in our ecosystem, unchallenged and unconcerned with the consequences of anything they did.

Now I know what you're thinking at this point in the narrative, but let me assuage you of your John Hughes 1980's fantasies—I was not, at that time, in love with Serafina. But it was an easy thing to mistake (which my sister did many, many times) because from the outside a lot of the male behaviors looked the same.

Case in point: we were always together, and that alone will alway get people talking. And we weren't just in each other's presence a lot, we looked like a couple—always laughing, always close, and touching a lot. As far as that last part, Fina was a toucher, so her hand was never far from gently touching my shoulder; her arms never far from around me when we said goodbye at the end of the day.

But another male behavior that made it hard to distinguish

friend from unrequited love was being protective. Let me clarify. I wasn't some over the top alpha male who threatened any dude who came near Fina. But when she ran headfirst towards these douche bags I didn't know how to act. I seriously wanted to fight each and every one of them, but assholes in high school were just infinite grains of sand, there'd always be more, and eventually my arms would get tired of swinging.

She dated Russell for a month, and when they very predictably broke up she transitioned seamlessly to douche numero dos. Justin lived a few blocks away, and was a full on burn out. Kid never met a weed containing receptacle that he didn't fall in love with. Fina grabbed him up right away—saw the two of them standing a little too close in the hallways and I knew what was up. That lasted as long as that was ever going to last, then she transitioned to that weird dude Jerome who was in the band. Not band like school band, he was in his own metal band, so he looked like what you're picturing. Long hair, dark attitude, the whole nine. That lasted a little longer than Justin—about a week or so—the equivalent of a three-year marriage and two kids in the dog years teen relationships were measured in.

After those ill-fated mistakes finally ended I assumed the crazy fog had lifted, but like I said she was gorgeous in ways that you have to experience to believe, and beauty like hers was a siren song that only horny high school assholes seemed to hear.

And after I had to sit back and watch all of these mistakes unfold, I started to notice something about myself. I went from being annoyed at the guys to being annoyed at Serafina, but I was too much of a pussy to confront her about her teenage co-dependence. I'd tell anyone else who would listen, including her brother.

"Dude, what the fuck is wrong with your sister?"

"Don't talk about her like that," Damien said, attempting to puff his chest out but really just sticking his fat stomach out a little further than it already protruded.

"Or what, you're gonna fight me?"

"I will, yes."

He sounded so assured that I had to smile. He meant it, the poor bastard. I guess that was sweet, but when you're a kid stuff like that just comes across as inadvertently funny.

"We'll put your obvious delusions on the back burner for the greater good. I'm not 'talking' about your sister. I'm worried about her. She seems to be good at finding every dickhead in our graduating class and hanging out with them. What's up with that?"

"You're asking me? We're not like you and Clover, dude. Girl's a mystery to me sometimes."

She was becoming a mystery to me too. One after the other she found them, and it became such a thing at school that Fina was getting something she hadn't accounted for—a reputation. In high school that shit stuck like Gorilla Glue, and she was making the rounds a little too much to avoid the designations that the other girls were starting to give her. Clover worked on the PR side of things as best she could, but she was too in her own head to really do much—she just didn't know enough people (or how to talk to them).

I allowed myself all the comforting, self-deluding explanations my brain would allow before I had to call bullshit on myself. *She's just too innocent to notice; they must have fooled her—run a game so tight that they convinced her that they were good guys when they were really snakes.* But as the months passed I had to allow for alternative explanations (aka, the truth). And that was the part that was the hardest—not just seeing her with bad guys, not just having to help pick up the pieces afterwards, and not just feeling helpless to steer a good friend back onto Sanity Road. The hardest part was the realization that Serafina was fucked up with a capital F, and no amount of help I could offer was going to change that.

That thought haunted me because it was so familiar, so I uncharacteristically pushed it off into the realm of denial, until I had no choice but to confront it, full on. I guess I have Russel to thank for that.

A LADY WHO MAY (OR, MORE LIKELY) MAY NOT HAVE BEEN ASSAULTED

The Meadows had its dark side, just like every other neighborhood. A few years before the stuff with Serafina happened, a woman was assaulted in one of the communal laundry rooms that sat adjacent to an apartment complex near our place. Those rooms have been filled in since, but in the 80's and 90's they were next to every apartment building in the complex—a supposed convenience so that people in the neighborhood didn't have to go to a laundromat a town over (like I said, we weren't those House Kids across the way—they had washers and dryers in their houses. To this day I find it weird that I don't have to go out to do laundry).

Picture a staircase leading to a subterranean room with shaky fluorescent lights that hung overhead, flickering and buzzing as they illuminated the three washers and dryers in the room. They were convenient and dangerous places, and after it rained they filled with the sort of unidentifiable and overly sized insects (imagine one of those super creatures from a bygone geological eon) that didn't fly in the traditional sense, but would make horrible noises as they coasted through the air for short distances, always towards you, always landing right by your feet.

That was why we avoided those places, even though, despite our parents continued anxiety for our safety, we did make it down there from time to time when we needed a really good hiding place for a game of Manhunt or Hide-and-Seek.

But the assault on that woman became a neighborhood urban legend. I don't know if it really happened, or if the idea of ferocious attacks perpetrated by strangers became our Bogeyman, a cautionary tale to keep children as safe as possible when the adults couldn't be around. It had all the trappings of a classic urban legend—the victim never had a name. It was always 'that woman', and despite the fact that the crime had occurred so close to where we lived, no one ever knew the alleged victim. No one recounted the statement they'd given police about what they'd heard or seen. No one ever remembered a wave of police cars on 73rd Avenue, where the laundromat in question sat, or seeing the victim being taken in the back of an ambulance. Nothing like that.

Even the details of the crime were sketchy, and it almost depended on which set of parents was telling it. The parents of the really bad kids—the ones always getting into trouble in school and out—told their kids the most extreme, borderline unbelievable version of the story. How did we know? Because those kids would repeat it at lunch in the cafeteria, and the extremity of the details was alway directly correlated to how bad of a person the kid doing the telling was.

Like Brandon. That kid was always spinning some crazy-ass tale, exaggerating to the point of non-believability, mostly because he craved some much-needed attention he wasn't getting at home. By the time the story of the Assaulted Woman was being recounted by him in gym class, that shit had taken on full out mythological elements. One woman being attacked by one man became a yarn about a gang turf war, a dispute over drugs (or guns, or. . . whatever gangs fight over, despite the fact that there were zero gangs where we lived).

Even when it wasn't being told by some miscreant at school, I always wondered about that story. Had parents decided to repeat the tale of the poor laundry mat assault victim to scare us? Did some of them actually believe it? Or did events actually go down as told?

I don't know, and I never will. But thinking of that story made me wonder about our neighborhood, and our parents. How they were always so worried about threats from outside. The strange man in the laundromat. The mysterious kidnapper who was sure to grab one of us if we dared walk home from school by ourselves instead of with our friends. They talked about that stuff constantly. All that concern for the external, but they never saw the real threats, the homegrown terror, the boys hiding in plain sight.

Maybe those dudes were out there, prowling the hood looking for women to assault, apartments to rob, and cars to break into—but I never met any of them. Despite how close we were to Manhattan (*close has to remain a relative term— while we were gps close to the City, the realities of driving in LIE traffic could make it a journey to rival Europeans sailing to the New World), crime was a rare thing. In eighteen years of living in The Meadows I remember one crime and one crime only—a car being broken into late at night, and it turned out to be a nineteen-year-old kid who'd regretted his decision to smash the car window and ran away.

What the kids knew and the adults forgot was that the real threats were internal. The real concern wasn't getting your car jacked, it was having your kid tortured by the neighbor's kid in science class. No one was kidnapping my ass, but the number of kids who'd hijacked my state of mind were legion, and there was never any guidance on how to navigate them. Here's what I knew:

1. **I knew to stop-drop-and roll should I spontaneously ignite.**
2. **I knew to always yell 'stranger danger' should some random adult try to lure me into his windowless van to 'help find his puppy.'**
3. **I knew to always say something if I saw something.**

Now, here are the things I did not know as well:

1. **I did not know who to talk to when my parents were too sick to be parents.**
2. **I did not know how to handle the growing concern that me and my sister might inherit some of whatever they have.**
3. **And I did not know how to navigate the Bastards of Queens—the homegrown threats that were really what we all needed to be worried about.**

Who were these boys? Kids like Russell. Kids like his shitty best friend (and my neighbor) Jared. Bad guys, making their list of who to terrorize next.

I always wondered if my great grandfather was one of them, I mean even before the disease took his brain. Was he just, like, a regular dude over in Greece when he was sixteen? Just a nice boy with dreams of the future? Or was he just a bastard without a victim? Maybe his parents beat the shit out of him and told him he was trash (this is a likelihood, being raised in that poor old-world environment, whatever we may think of it from a modern viewpoint).

I don't know the answer and I never will, for Thomas or for The Bastards of Queens, but after a while I stopped wondering about their origin stories and started worrying about the people they were hurting.

This is the point in our story where Russell re-emerges to fuck things up one more time.

OUR FIRST FIGHT

When it comes to close friends there are fights, and there are *fights*. Serafina and I had a fight-fight the day she sat across from me in the cafeteria to tell me she was giving Russell a second chance. We all had the same lunch period— period 5 –that weird high school thing where you eat lunch before noon. I never ate much, not only because the school lunch was a step above that wet cat food that comes in cans with a picture of a salmon on it, but also because I was never hungry at that time of day. This left me with less in my mouth, and therefore more to say than anyone else. My thoughts weren't always well received, especially when they were laced with venomous judgement.

"Wait, what the hell are you talking about?"

Clover and Carmine looked at me with a that 'oh shit' expression on their faces. Those were fighting words I'd just said, but by that point I'd grown so incredulous at what I perceived as her stupid behavior when it came to guys, that I was ready for a confrontation if need be. I was willing to accept a two-week indiscretion and file it under 'girls have to date assholes at some point in their lives', but this was something else. This wasn't Girl-Dates-Asshole. This was Girl-Dates-Asshole, realizes that he's a bad guy, lets some time pass, then goes back to said Asshole. It made no sense.

"What are you talking about?" Serafina looked up from her. . . I think it was one of those gross high school cafeteria chicken sandwiches, but who knows. I could hear the 'I'm ready to fight' in her voice.

"You're seriously going back out with that D bag?"

"Don't call him that," she said. It was the wrong thing for her to say to me. Not only was she going out with him, now she was defending him. Carmine jumped in to be the voice of reason.

"Fina, we've known Russell a long time. Trust me, D bag is actually the nicest thing any of us have to say about him. He's a dick. He's the king of the dicks."

"Well you don't know him like I do, then. I see a different side of him."

"Fina," Clover jumped in. "That might be, but he broke up with you, remember? You felt like shit and he didn't care at all."

That's when 5th period lunch became a full out episode of Intervention—Dating Assholes Edition. Each of us took turns trying to not so gently point out all of the reasons Russell wasn't the nicest of human beings. One by one we went through his Greatest Hits album. I told her about the time I saw him throw a rock at a birds' nest full of babies when we were seven. Carmine told her about the time he threw a lit cigarette into a dry bush that sat next to an apartment building just so he could watch the fire. On and on we went. None of it seemed to penetrate the co-dependent forcefield Fina had built around herself.

"Look, I get it, but all of that was a long time ago, right?

Years and years ago, so what does that have to do with him now?"

I couldn't believe what I was hearing. I was getting more mad with each passing rationalization she made. I remember that moment as being the first time I looked at her differently —not with judgment, exactly, but with the knowledge that she wasn't just my quirky friend—she was messed up in ways that were already manifesting in ways clear enough for a whole table full of teenagers to recognize.

"Can I ask you a question?"

"Sure." She put down her sandwich and folded her hands in an almost sarcastic way. "Ask away."

"Do you think that he just changed? For real, do you think he was this awful kid who liked hurting things, and then one day, poof, he was a nice person? 'Cause we haven't even told you the worst of him, and you sound like his lawyer and you barely know the kid. Why is that?"

This was the point in the conversation that she decided she was done. I'd never really seen people outside of TV shows walk away in the middle of a conversation. As screwed up as my family was—and it was—we always talked things out. I guess they didn't do that in the Gilmore household, because after I asked what I thought was a perfectly reasonable question she pushed her lunch tray aside and stormed off.

"Well that went well, huh?"

"Shut up, Carmine."

"That was. . . rough." I could tell that Clover was disturbed by the whole interaction. It was one thing for boys to tell a girl she was dating a bad guy, but it was another for a female friend to do the same and have her concerns ignored.

"Yeah it was," I agreed. I didn't know what to do next. Like I said, people storming off in anger were uncharted waters for me, so I just sat there while everyone else finished their French fries.

The school day ended, and I walked home with Carmine, Clover, and Damien. Normally Serafina would have joined us —we always went home together—but as we joined the rush of bodies on the giant lawn outside of the school at 2:45, I saw Fina holding hands with Russell as they walked into the horizon.

For a while after that I gave up on my friendship with Serafina. I doubt that I saw it in these terms back then, but I think the idea of a great girl, who I loved being with a piece of shit was a little too familiar for me. Every woman I knew at the time had done the same. It was the story of my family, the reason things were the way they were, and Serafina seemed like the latest in a long line of women who did things that made no sense to me. I was starting to be mad at them all, even though I had no business being feeling like that.

I guess you had to understand where Fina and Damien came from—their home life—to fully understand the ways their damage manifested. I never knew it intimately, but I can tell you what I saw, and you can make of it what you choose.

THE UNFORTUNATE FATE OF TWO
GREY SQUIRRELS

You remember our little neighborhood greeting from earlier, right? And how Hank did his best to not let us inside? Well I found out why he was so gun shy about having people in his duplex. In the summertime, we spent our days on the basketball court. Carmine and I had gotten sick of playing each other and whatever randoms came by looking for a game, so having another kid in the area we could add to our never-ending game of roundball was just fine with us. Within a few weeks we had a pretty established routine of getting Damien up so that we could claim the court before the older kids showed up with their crews and pushed us off.

"Yo, Colorblind!" we yelled at his bedroom window one morning. His yard had a large wooden fence, like all of our backyards did, but we just opened it and walked right up to his back door. On that day, though, we just yelled. This was a time before cell phones, if that's even possible to conceive of, so to get the group together we'd just walk up to each other's windows and either shout (my personal preference), or try the front-door route. The front always came with risks, like cranky parents who'd already conceived of the menial chores their kids should be doing instead of shooting hoops. So, windows it was.

"You think he's still asleep?" Carmine asked me after our yells got no response.

"Maybe. You never know. Might have been up all night watching old Summer Slams."

We both laughed hysterically. To describe Damien as a hardcore professional wrestling fan would have been like describing my parents as just a little eccentric. The kid worshiped at the alter of Hulk Hogan, the Ultimate Warrior, and Shawn Michaels. He loved wrestling so much that Carmine and I had to tell him when to tone it down in public, because the kid would meet a girl and start going on about who was fighting in the next Survivor Series without thinking twice about it.

"Colorblind, let's go, get your lazy ass up already!"

We called him colorblind because of how he dressed. He looked like what he was—a kid with no mom—because there isn't a mother alive who'd let their son walk out of the house in some of the get ups he rocked with almost no awareness of how strange he looked. Nothing he wore matched. He'd wear white undershirts underneath multi-colored jerseys, paired with sneakers that had weird patterns on them and pants that didn't include any of the colors on anything else he was wearing. On top of that, he wore his house keys around his neck on a chain, sometimes tucked under his shirt and sometimes just hanging down to his stomach, which bulged out of his body like a puppy who'd gotten into an open bag of kibble and eaten himself stupid.

Then there were the hats—too many of the damn things to keep track of. They never quite fit his head, and they were always sports teams that he knew nothing about. He'd come out in a new Yankees cap even though I'm pretty sure he never saw a baseball game in his life. The next day it would the Red Sox—and he never realized the sacrilege. It was like he went on some crazed and random shopping spree at Modells. His clothing was a metaphor, a representation of his home life—disorganized, off center, and more than a little bit sad.

"There he is. He's pulling up the blinds now." Carmine nudged me as we saw Damien appear in his window in nothing but the old, stained white undershirt he seemed to wear at least three times a week. He put his finger over his mouth as if to tell us to shut the hell up, then disappeared back into his room. This was our signal to each other in a time before you could just text your friends to come outside.

Like clockwork, he came out ten minutes later, looking his usual mess. Carmine would miss no chance to fuck with him. "You really earn your nickname some days, man. We would have gladly waited another few minutes while you took the time to match your damn clothing."

"Fuck you guys, I look fine."

"Yeah," I said, jumping in to make the kid feel just a little bit worse. "If by 'fine' you mean fucked up and colorblind, then yeah, you look awesome."

"You know I hate it when you guys call me that."

"We know," I said. "That's why we do it. That, and you really are colorblind, Jesus." He punched me in the shoulder, weakly, which I totally deserved. Then we laughed like we always did after a round of giving each other shit. "You know your sister's at my house already? Think her and Clover had a sleepover."

"I heard her get up but I didn't know where she was going. She's been wandering a lot lately."

"Wandering? What do you mean?"

"I mean wandering. She leaves the house and tells Dad

that she'll be back later, but she never says where she's going. Then a few hours later she's back, and she never talks about where she went or what she did."

"That sounds weird, man," Carmine said. "You never ask?"

"I ask all the time, but she never tells me. You know how girls are, they have secrets. It's easier just let it go sometimes. But enough about my sister. We playing, or what?"

"We're playing, you're losing," I joked. "We can go through the motions if you want, but you know how it's gonna turn out."

"I might surprise you," he answered. We laughed again, which only made him angrier.

"Hey, you guys wanna get food before we play?" Carmine asked.

"I don't even think the pizza place is open yet."

"So we can get some shit from the candy store," I said.

"I'm not hungry, why don't we just play?" This was Damien-speak for *I don't have a dollar to my name*. None of us were anything close to rich, but even among the middle-class families that made up our neighborhood, the Gilmores were the poor ones. They could pay the rent on their duplex, but that was about it.

Damien never had money for anything, not even the slice of pizza we got almost every day after school. Back then slices were less than two dollars, but even that price point was an issue for him. Carmine and I would take out the five-dollar bills that our parents had given us, and Damien would reach into his mismatched shorts to pull out a bunch of pennies and some lint from the dryer. If it was a good day, he might have a few quarters buried there, but it was almost never a good day.

Being with him at those moments could be embarrassing.

We'd all be at the pizza place ordering a few slices, and as Carmine and I handed our five-dollar bills to the guy, Damien would stack a pile of nickels and dimes on the counter, one at a time, like an old lady at the grocery store. What's worse, he never had enough for anything we wanted to do, and, more often than not, we had to cover his food and drink with the change from our fives. But we felt pity for him, even though we each had our own shit going on. Why? Well, if you knew his dad a little better, like we did, you'd understand why.

Hank Gilmore worked for one of the largest cable companies on the East coast, but not exactly on the business side of things. He was a cable-guy—the person who came to your house and wired shit up so you could finally get HBO. They didn't have a car of their own, just the company van that I was pretty sure he wasn't supposed to use as his own personal vehicle. It always sat there, beaten up as everything else the Gilmores had, parked in front of their duplex, rusting away—a metaphor for what was happening inside of their home.

Hank looked a hot mess most days. He had a perpetual five o'clock shadow that revealed flecks of black and grey in his beard, and his hair was always a mess, the odor of cigarettes and beer stayed on him like PigPen. Even though we all had screwy parents in one way or another, our folks were generally polite to our friends. All except Hank. He was a prick, and he had weird rules the kids had to follow.

No one was allowed in their duplex, for one. That might make it sound like he was just a private guy, but you have to understand the culture of the neighborhood back then. We came and went in each other's homes all day, every day. We called each other's parents 'Mom' or 'Dad' half the time out of habit. Our house in particular had always been a home base for all the neighborhood kids since we were little, even the ones we no longer hung out with by the time high school came around. We had the coolest toys, the latest video games (Mom spoiled us when she could), and the coolest mom around. As time went on and Mom got sicker, that all faded, but as long as I could remember it was *nuestra casa es su casa.*

Not so much for the Gilmores. For Hank it was a hard and fast rule that his kid's friends (i.e., us) stay out at all times. But like all rules, we found ways around it. I remember the first time I went into that hell hole of a duplex. After a few hours of ball, I walked Damien back to his place, and when we got to his back door (Damien always went through the back, never through the front) I asked if I could have a drink.

"I'll bring it out to you," he told me.

"Why? Just let me come in and grab it."

He looked at me like he was already in trouble, even though no rules had been violated just yet. "I'm not supposed to."

"Supposed to what? Give your friends drinks?"

"Have people over when my dad's not here. He's kind of strict about it."

"Oh," I said, finding the whole thing weird. "Why not?"

"I don't know, he never says why. I just know that me and Fina aren't supposed to have anyone over."

"That's fine, then. You can bring it out to me. It's cool."

It was at that moment that I first saw some of the anger and resentment that Damien had built up for his dad. It wasn't so obvious, but I saw it in his eyes. He wanted to break his dad's stupid rules, not because he was a defiant kid, but because he didn't like how controlling his father was. "Nah, fuck it, man, come in and get it. Just don't tell him or he'll have my ass."

"My lips are sealed."

The second I stepped through the door I realized why Hank didn't want anyone in there. It was like they were homeless, only they had walls and a roof, and complimentary cable. There was trash all over the floor, mostly discarded pizza boxes from Meadows Pizza and crumpled fast food bags. But it wasn't my eyes that were on high alert when I walked through the doorway, it was my nose. The place stank in a way that was hard to describe because it was a combination of so many different bad smells. They all seemed to merge together into their own melodious stench.

My mom used to be into cooking shows, and I remember watching episodes with her where the contestants would have a challenge to taste a dish and try to tell all of the ingredients that had gone into it. I was having an experience like that, only instead of trying to parse out whether a dish had cilantro in it, I was trying to tell if the assault on my nostrils was being committed by rotting food, spilled beer, or overly filled ashtrays.

"Follow me," Damien said, leading me to the kitchen.

"You got it."

I felt like I was at a crime scene, taking in every single detail like a detective trying to solve the what-the-fuck-happened-here mystery. In the ten steps it took to get from back door to fridge I noticed the following things, in no particular order.

1. A piece of pizza crust next to the TV stand. There was a little bit of congealed cheese and nasty looking sauce still on it. The pizza box sat on the coffee table adjacent to their TV.
2. There were at least six open beer cans, and that's just what I could count as I walked.
3. Hank had three different ashtrays in one room, and

each looked like urns worth of cremated bodies
had been dumped into them. They were so full
that whole areas of the floor beneath them were
covered in this thin grey layer where the ashes had
fluttered to the ground, uncleaned.

Once we got to the kitchen it was even worse, if that were imaginable. As Damien opened up the fridge to get me a cold bottle of water, I took a quick and unfortunate glance around the room. Now, messy is one thing—I had messes in my house that my parents were always nagging me to clean—but dirty was another thing entirely. Dirty was unsanitary. Dirty was total apathy. Dirty always seemed to involve old food. And in Hank's case, it was a pile of dishes so high that it actually rose above the lip of the sink like some kind of twisted modern art project, half eaten food and all. There wasn't even water soaking anything. It was as if every night, for god-knows-how-many nights, Hank ate a full meal and then put his plate in the sink, then forgot he'd done that. Rinse and repeat.

"Here you go."

"Thanks." I remember trying to hide the shock I was feeling by not making eye contact. And I just kept drinking to avoid having to talk. I drank so fast that my stomach started to hurt.

"Jeez, you really were thirsty, damn."

"Uh-huh."

Afterwards I thanked him for the water and got the hell out of there as fast as I could. I was so worried that when I got back to my house everyone was going to ask me what the hell that awful smell on me was, but I guess it abated in the open air between his duplex and mine. That had been my introduction to the Gilmore's way of life. I didn't want to make too much of it, didn't want to think that just because their house was a mess that Hank's parenting had to be a mess also, but I couldn't fight the thought off. Then I thought of my own house, and how the places each of us lived represented something larger. If the home my mom grew up in was a façade put up for visitors, ours was the opposite— our homes were exactly as they appeared.

The Gilmores lived like pigs. Carmine's place was dark and detached. And as far as Clover and I went, well, it was complicated. Depending on the day and time someone came over, they got a glimpse into one of the many versions of our lives. Sometimes it was perfectly normal—Mom greeted people, they said hello, she offered and got them drinks or food, all that. Other times she was hiding in her room like that house cat who you know lives there, but is always hiding in somewhere you can't locate.

"Okay," we said after realizing he had no money for food. "Let's just play." I grabbed the ball. "We can probably get a few games in before anyone else shows up."

"What are we playing to?" Damien asked.

"Eleven," I said. "Are you new? Always eleven. Gotta win by two."

The 'gotta win by two part' always kept our basketball games going longer than an eleven point game sounded like it might go, and that was just fine with us. We liked to keep our own little informal records of wins and losses (Damien always had a losing one), but really what we liked to do was get out of our houses and be around one another as much as possible. It didn't matter if the court was uneven (which it was), it didn't matter if the net was missing from the rim (it was stolen by some ghetto kids who lived a few blocks over), and it really didn't matter that none of us were particularly good basketball players. We played, and we played for as long as we could until something interrupted us.

That day, it was Hank who interrupted.

"DAMIEN!" The sound of his yell was deep and imposing, and even though we were really far away Hank sounded like he was standing next to us, screaming in our ears. "GET OVER HERE!" Damien snapped to attention like he was a cadet in basic training. Literally, his back straightened, and he dropped the ball he'd been holding onto. As it rolled away down the uneven pavement he turned to us with disappointment in his eyes.

"I gotta go guys, sorry."

"Wait, are you coming back?"

"Yeah, Dad just likes to know where I am. He wants me to check in."

"Check in?" Carmine asked sarcastically. "Dude, we're right here. He can obviously see us, and you've only been out here like twenty minutes."

"I know," he answered, sounding defeated. "It's just how he is. I can't change it. Lemme go deal with this."

"Alright, we'll meet you in the park."

The park was about 50 feet from the court, and sat adjacent to the Gilmore's duplex. We shot a few more times, then made our way over and sat on the swings that faced his place. Carmine looked annoyed. "This is so dumb. Check in? We're in our own backyard—he can see us!"

"I know, man, but like Damien said, it is what it is. We can keep ourselves busy until he comes out."

"We should go wait in his yard."

"Wait, why?"

"Because it'll make it clear to his dad that he interrupted us. You know, like put pressure on him to do his little check in faster."

"Two things. First, that's a stupid idea. And second, I think you're just jealous. My two cents."

Carmine looked at me angrily. "Me? Jealous? Of what?"

"Aren't you the one always going on about how no one cares about you? That you stay out late and no one in your family comes to look for you? I think you secretly wished that you had to check in with your dad. Don't take your frustration out on Damien, he can't do anything about how his parents are. None of us can." It was one of those checkmate moments where he had nothing to say back to me because he knew that I was right. He'd have cut off his right arm to have to check in like Damien was doing.

"Whatever, man. But I'm going to go throw this away in his yard. We can head over there, maybe he'll be done in a minute." Carmine put the last piece of Big Red gum into his mouth and scrunched up the wrapper. "You coming?"

I rolled my eyes and followed. A few feet and we were on the old wooden planks that made up Damien's yard—an ill-conceived attempt at a deck that now made his yard look like an old rotting pirate ship. Near his back door was a large black garbage can whose lid was always on. That should have been our first clue that something was up. The blinds were closed, as was the back door, but I could still hear the yelling inside. It sounded like the ranting of a drunk—slurred words, things that don't make sense. I held my hand up to stop Carmine from knocking on the door.

"Hold up, man, you hear that?"

All I could imagine was Damien, probably standing there with his head faced towards the ground, his shoulders rounded, a tear forming in his eye. He was a soft kid—not made from iron whatsoever, and now I was starting to see why.

"Is everyone's dad a complete asshole?"

"That's a hard question to answer," I said. "But his definitely is."

Carmine took another step forward and I went to hold him back again. "I'm not going to interrupt the lecture, I just need to throw this away." I moved my hand and he stepped forward. As the yelling continued inside, Carmine lifted the never-missing top from the garbage can, and what was inside made me almost vomit.

The can was full of rainwater, and it had to have been old because it hadn't rained in at least two weeks. But the smell of brackish, stagnant water wasn't what almost made me vomit. That prize went to the two very large, very dead grey squirrels who were floating, half rotten, at the top of their watery little graves. The smell was overwhelming; Carmine and I jumped back yelling a mutual 'oh shit' in perfect harmony. He slammed the lid right back down as we heard the creak of the back door reopening.

"Guys I can't come out right now, my dad needs me to clean up a little."

I could tell that Damien was holding back tears. I didn't want him to feel worse than he already did. "No problem, man. We'll be out here a while so if you finish your chores just come find us, okay."

"Thanks. Later."

"Later."

This story has been a running joke between Carmine and I. Almost every time I see him now we try to figure out the logistics of the two dead squirrels. Did they climb in and get caught in the rain? That didn't seem likely. Was the can already full of water and they stumbled in and drowned? No scenario made sense, so we went to less plausible but more interesting ones. Did Hank kill the squirrels and dump them in there and just leave them? We never figured it out, and we sure as shit never asked. It was more fun to make shit up. Needless to say, we avoided his yard after that.

In hindsight, that experience has a greater significance than just being a funny thing that happened when we were kids. The two dead squirrels represented neglect. They represented a lack of care. Those two squirrels were metaphors for Hank's parenting and Damien's upbringing. It was easy enough to see what his home and his father had done to the poor kid. He was insecure, he was scared, he was lonely. But Serafina was a different story—the Lisa Simpson of the Gilmore family—her issues manifested in different ways, and I always struggled to understand her place in that family. Maybe her mother had been the normal one, who knows. If so, I hope Fina took after her, but the more time I spent around her the less likely that seemed. As we left school and I saw Fina's fingers interlocked with Russell's, I started to realize that there was no such thing as normal if you were in the Sick Parents Club. Serafina was just another messed up girl looking for love in the wrong places. She wasn't alone, she was a product of her environment like all the rest of us.

It wasn't a question of whether or not we were damaged —the only a question was how each of us handled it.

INTERLUDE

Three Women
1939-1996

CONTINENTS WORTH OF COUNTRIES

I liked to draw, even though I was terrible at it. It was therapy for me, a way to pretend that I was a comic artist even though I would never be the Chris Claremont's and Todd McFarlane's of this world, much to my chagrin. Even though my drawing skills were trash, it was fun to make up my own comic book adventures—to pretend, for however long, that I had control over a world gone mad. In the real world things were chaos, unpredictable. But over my made up cities and heroes I had control. There the bad guys never won. There the world made sense. Mostly I drew by myself, but sometimes I cut Carmine in on that action—we had a whole storyline of a character named Captain Justice, who was like this fucked up, poorly drawn Queens version of Captain America, only his feet pointed in the same direction because, like I said, our drawings were trash.

When not collaborating with my best friend, I mostly drew alone, but every now and then my sister caught me.

"What are you doing?" Clover asked when she came in one day to find me hunched over a pad I'd gotten at this art store Mom used to take me to on Union Turnpike. My impulse was to put my arms around my shitty drawing and bare my teeth like an unsocialized dog, but I realized she wasn't just being a pestering sister, she was actually interested in what I was doing.

Drawing, I answered.

This inevitably begged follow up questions, stopping me from finishing my masterpiece.

Drawing what?

Just come look, I told her, it's easier to show you than to tell you.

Clover stood over me as I sat at the desk in my room. It was too fancy of a desk for a kid, but so was all of the furniture in my room. Our grandmother Eleni was many things, but cheap she was not. Her and the finer things in life were peanut butter and chocolate—the immigrant daughter's revenge for a childhood spent with parents who treated frugality as a virtue. worshiping at the altar of frugality.It wasn't just my room, either. Our whole place was filled with furniture that my parents never would have bought (and probably couldn't afford) on their own. That's where I sat and compose my masterpieces. That's where I still sit to write today. But back to the past. . .

What are you drawing? Is that . . .

Mom, yeah. It's Mom.

Is she. . .

Wearing a cape? Yes, shut up.

I didn't even say anything!

I know, but you were going to.

I was, but it wasn't going to be anything bad. Who's that with her? There are three of them.

They're a trio, I explained. A three person team.

You made Mom into a superhero?

She already is, I thought. I just gave her a cooler outfit than the sweatpants she never takes off anymore.

Yeah. Her and grandma and great-grandma. They fight together.

Who do they fight? Criminals, like Batman?

I forgave my sister for speaking of DC characters in my presences—she knew not what she did.

No, I told her. No criminals—they're not like Batman. Well, sort of, I guess.

What do you mean?

I mean they fight, but not crime. Not robbers and killers.

Then who, Clover asked.

Bad men, I told her, The Men Who Hurt.

She just looked at me like I was nuts, then said 'oh, okay' before going back to studying or whatever she was doing at the time. I kept drawing. This was issue number 2—a critical one in any series. The origin story was still being written.

It's the story of three women—all of whom are needed to tell this story properly, as it needs to be told. There's a line that runs through them all, like a strand of unwoven DNA, crossing time and space, connecting Kalamata to my tiny room in Queens. Let me tell you about them.

The first of these women—and only designated as the first because I know of no one before her—had the misfortune of being the most obviously victimized of them all. Her death—and more specifically the manner of her death—erased from record any semblance of humanity she might have had for me. Her victimhood became a master status, transforming her from Angelikh, my great grandmother, to Angela The Murdered. What was lost to history were those things that made her who she was: her favorite tea; her dreams of the future; the way she reacted when one of her babies woke up crying late at night; the things that made her Angela, before her husband ended all of her possibilities.

The rest of her story—the before the murder part—is long gone, along with anyone who possessed memories of that genealogical epoch. It was her oldest daughter, my grandmother, who would set the course of my family's future even more directly—the Michael Corleone to Angela's Vito.

Eleni enters our narrative in the most dramatic fashion— fighting off (quite literally) a filicidal patriarch gone mad with disease. The details remain sketchy, but somehow, someway she subdued her murderous father long enough for the police to be called. He was tried and convicted of murder, committed to a mental institution for the criminally insane, and spent his handful of remaining years slowly and painfully dying, alone and unvisited by friend or relation alike. He was buried in a potters field for the indigent, alongside the rest of the lunatics whose families made no claim to their former loved ones remains, and there he remains, unconsecrated.

But back to his firstborn—the one left to clean up the mess of all messes. Eleni decided to rebrand the concept of victim, and give it a much needed new logo. No degree of dead mother or psychotic father was going to bend the iron that woman had running though her. Of what words or experiences that iron was forged in is unknown, but it was surely there, in every survived trauma, in the way she comported herself all of her days—the look of survival she'd pass on to her daughter one day.

These days they'd say she had grit— progressives would declare her a feminist heroine, we'd hashtag her struggles in our tweets. W e'd check her Instagram several times a day for inspiration to help us through the bad times.

But as it was, there were no Hollywood directors waiting outside of her Queens apartment to capture Eleni's story. No paparazzi. No vloggers. There were only early mornings and late nights—second and third shifts—the life of raising her mother and father's children.

Although she'd live deep into her 80's, Eleni learned that hardness had its price. Among other things, that price included the existence of anything warm and fuzzy that may have once existed inside of her taking a back seat to the subtle act of getting shit done—a thing she did like no other.

In summary, the good: before breathing her last, she raised her parents' children as well as she could and ultimately worked three full careers, the last of which she was the Boss (yes, a capital B is required in this case). Once in a position of power—something she seemed almost destined for, she used it to lift up those in whom she saw aspects of her own life—the immigrant women, the mothers, those who needed a helping hand to progress. And when she died, those women who, like Eleni's own mother, has traversed continents worth of countries so that their babies would live a life free from the constraints of the past, showed up in droves to pay their respects. It was the least that they could do.

And now, of course, the bad: while Eleni shared all of her mother's toughness and determination, genetics aren't that simple—you don't get just the cool shit and nothing else. With the aspects of her personality that kept her alive when dying made more sense, came her mother's proclivity to marry the wrong man. Another hurter. Another bad guy, only this one we imported from another family. His victim was my mother, and upon her he visited all of the unspeakable trauma that a man can to a little girl.

A little before I came into the world, my scumbag abusive grandfather took his very last inhale of oxygen before dying a remarried old man somewhere in Florida. Eleni went on, as she always had, moving in two blocks away from us in the

Meadows, living with her younger sister for the rest of her life. That immigrant daughter's work ethic stayed with her until the end, only leaving her when cancer (yet again) robbed her body of its willingness to work. Then and only then.

But for the decades before, her life was characterized by taking the bus every damn day and changing the lives of strangers more than she ever could her own children. On that score—the parent score— she earned a Satisfactory at best. Lost points for marrying an abusive man. Lost points for denying his villainy with each passing breath. Lost points for not recognizing the damage done to her own baby girl.

But like every woman in my family, Mom had that iron inside of her. When I think of it I remember what it was that I loved so much about comics. The best Superheros—the ones I stayed up late reading about—all had something in common: they were perfectly ordinary. Pedestrian. Your average Jane. Only they went through something—the bite of a radioactive spider, a bath in gamma rays, whatever. And that whatever—that transformative moment—made them into something much greater than what they had been before. That was my mom. Transformed at a young age, but what she became was something magical.

When we were little, she shared in her family tradition of taking care of others, becoming the neighborhood Mom to all the kids with sick parents. Everyone came over our house to hang out. Mom would make them food, she'd help them with their homework if they needed, she'd let them exist as they were in a world where that wasn't always a possibility. That was her gift. That's what my friends still remember her for.

If you saw her back then you'd never believe that she would be the most fragile person I'd ever known, but as I came to learn throughout my childhood and adolescence, that's what the disease does, it breaks down even the strongest over time. It crumbles mountains one pebble at a time.

But before all that—before the sadness that came later—she was a rock, a survivor of her own childhood. But the ultimate expression of her strength wasn't just in raising us despite the demons I now know she was wrestling with, but in one of her greatest acts of accomplishment—going back to school. This might sound trivial, but I promise you that it was anything but. Mom was an intellectual at heart, a writer and a philosopher, but she never made it through college the first time around because her demons chased her all the way to Michigan—the place she tried to escape that home of hers—the place she tired to put the previous eighteen years of her life squarely behind her. As she quickly learned—what all haunted people eventually learned—was that there was no bus ticket you could buy to escape the demons that lived inside. Those fuckers would always catch you.

Shaking, Crying, Sadness, Dropping Out. Get a job, get married, have some kids. That was life up to that point, but it had always been a dream to go back, to get that elusive degree that had been denied her when she was younger, and that's exactly what she did. Not only did she graduate, but she even entered an essay competition and won the damn thing. I still have that essay. It's the only thing I have left of hers. I'll let her speak in her own words.

I didn't begin to write until I returned to college after my children began junior high school. My writing was confined to course requirements; I had no sense of my own style or voice, having been too well indoctrinated with the precepts of English teachers who implicitly taught that my writing should echo their speech.

I was fortunate to take a course with an English professor who considered my writing to be of a quality worth developing, and he encouraged me to take my writing more seriously. I realized that it was not just the imitative writing style I'd been taught that had dulled me, but that traces of low self-esteem had kept me from freeing my imagination and aptitude. Here was a revelation: I understood that it was not only possible, but essential for me to find my own voice, my own style and my own material. I began to work at my writing with the same diligence and earnestness I applied to motherhood.

My writing now expresses far more of the person I understand myself to be. Like James Baldwin, who remarks that he would forgo reliving the bleak fantasy of his childhood, I would not consider living my youth again. It is nevertheless a wellspring of material far more bearable in the telling than the living; I am the writer Cynthia Ozick characterizes as having been buffeted into being by life's ambushes. But I'm finally able to write about that life without fear of my family's censure or derision. It's exhilarating not to worry about my mother's self-exculpatory disclaimers concerning the accuracy of my memories. In much the same way Joan Didion maintains that the distinction between what actually happened and what could have happened is irrelevant, I, too, assert that remembering what it felt like to me, what it meant to be me, is the essence of what matters.

Translating the substance of my thoughts into words and onto paper starts with visualizing, then following the images on and on, until I contain them with words. Sometimes an idea surfaces when I'm at the point of consciousness intersecting wakefulness and sleep. I used to spring from bed, exclaiming in too loud a voice, "I have to write this down," waking my husband and kids as I charged downstairs to put my thoughts on paper. My son has thoughtfully provided me with pen and paper, placing them inside a small writing desk in a corner of my bedroom, which, ironically, I never use for writing.

Usually, though, the writing process begins when I'm able to find some time alone. I have a corner of my own. I sit in my Queen Anne chair with its worn brocade upholstery, set at an angle so that it faces the living room windows. My overweight cat wedges next to me, though there isn't enough room for both of us. Sitting in my old chair, lulled by the rhythm of my cat's purring, I stare out at an expanse of acreage that lies beyond my yard.

I watch the birds gather at the feeders I've set out, and recall a time when I was in my yard, standing very still, and an intrepid chickadee landed on my outstretched arm and ate seed from the palm of my hand. He came so close I could see the subtle shadings of his velvety black, gray and white feathers. Each time he husked a seed, he cocked his head to the side and looked at me, his eyes dark orbs of composed curiosity. I'm happy to see a male cardinal who returns each year, usually with a son, an immature male not yet as large or as red as the father, showing the young bird where food may be found. The older cardinal shows his son how to negotiate the congregation of birds—sparrows, starlings, juncos, tufted titmice, finches and black-capped chickadees—all vying for space on the feeders or for the mixed seed and pieces of suet strewn on the ground. Even their bird babble doesn't disturb my dozing cat.

Over the weather-worn pickets I see a scattering of oaks and pines, their limbs ornamented by the iridescence of the starlings' feathers. Crows, squirrels and mourning doves forage along the ground, the doves abruptly poising for flight when the territorial crows draw too near. An aged oak, badly damaged but not destroyed by lightning, stands on an upgrade, a sapling rising beneath its gnarled limbs. In the distance a copse to lilac trees marks a turn in the path; I cannot see what lies around the bend.

Although Annie Dillard seeks out ascetic workplaces in which to write, I prefer my niche. The well-worn chair, the softness of my cat's fur and the warmth of his closeness, and the activity and charm of the natural world I see through my windows, create a setting for imagining, thinking and writing.

At that same time that I write about the events and ordeals of my past, I also grow away from the experiences. I feel an invigorating and compelling pull outward, while more clearly understanding what James Baldwin sees as the writer's primary concern: to recreate out of the disorder of life the order which is art. The energy and effort invested in my writing, even the pain its delivery engenders, much like the birth of a child, are rewarded by a written work that is taken from me, but lives quite well on its own.

Drawing from the well of my past experiences, I recently wrote about my childhood home, which to the visitor's eyes was a place of comfort, tranquility and family harmony. Throughout my school years it was the place where my friends preferred to gather, always remarking how fortunate I was to have such a wonderful home and a mother who was the perfect hostess, welcoming and generous.

When my friends came into my home, they saw a living room dominated by a plush deep-cushioned couch, custom-made to accommodate one entire wall, with an eclectic collection of lithographs, oils, and sculptures above it. Companion armchairs with side tables were arranged in the corners of the room. A large teakwood table, surrounded by six chairs upholstered in raw silk, stood in the middle of the adjoining dining room. A matching sideboard, with a large beveled mirror hanging above it, was positioned against one wall. Bookcases filled the other two walls. Muted gold wall-to-wall carpeting covered the floors of both rooms.

Yet when the family was alone, we did not use the living or dining rooms. We could not sit on the couch or chairs. We could not eat at the table. Books could not be removed from their shelves without my mother's permission. Our shoes had to be removed before walking on the carpet when passing through these rooms. After my friends left, I was relegated to my room or to a dreary basement with its wood and tattered furnishings. My well-appointed home and ideal mother were facades masking instability and dysfunction. By continuing a pattern my mother had witnessed in her own family, she bequeathed to me a grievous legacy, one that I would have to overcome in order to rebuild my life and to secure a healthier inheritance for my own children.

I learned as a very young child that my mother experienced occasional psychotic episodes of violent behavior. But because these outbursts followed no particular pattern, I never knew when or how her irrational behavior would manifest itself. One quiet Saturday afternoon when I was twelve years old, I was sitting in my room, reading. No one was home except my mother and me. I had heard my mother coming up and going down the stairs several times, but, as I was engrossed in the book, the rhythm of her footsteps soon blended into the background of my thoughts. After a while my mother called to me, telling me to come into the bathroom.

When I walked in, the air was thick with steam, the walls sweating and the mirror fogged. On the floor, tipped over, was a small bucket. My mother had filled the tub halfway with pungent smelling boiling water of a yellowish color. She gripped my upper arms and turned me toward her until I was directly facing her. With an old fear I looked up into her face,

135

now transformed, and saw her flat expressionless eyes, her slack facial muscles. As her grip pinched tighter and more painfully, she told me, in a dulled tone, that I had to get into the tub. I flinched, trying to turn away, but I could not break her hold.

She pushed me backward against the wall, my shoulder blades pressed into a towel rack. She brought her left arm up and across my throat, forcing me up on my toes, while she tore at my clothes with her right hand. "Get in," she said more insistently. "You know you have to do this." Moving with unexpected speed and agility, she grabbed me again by my upper arms, swung me around and, without letting go, shoved me backward against the side of the tub. Still gripping me, she leaned me over the edge and into the scalding water. I passed out almost immediately.

When I regained consciousness, my mother was on her knees, her upper body stretched over the side of the tub. Her left arm cradled my neck; her right arm supported my back so I wouldn't slide under the water. "I used to do this for my mother," she said with a rigid smile. "She had six children, five of them lived, and the doctors told her she shouldn't have any more." I had, in fact, heard this story before. What I didn't know then was that my grandmother, who was later murdered by my grandfather, had made my mother participate in abortions performed at home, using a homemade abortive agent. One of the ingredients was powdered mustard; this accounted for the color and smell of the water. During her psychotic episodes, my mother sometimes thought I was other people. This time, initially, she spoke to me as if I was her mother, and although she now recognized me, she continued to behave the way she had with her mother. Looking into my eyes, the smile now gone, she went on in a sardonic tone. "But my father wouldn't leave her

alone. So whenever she'd get pregnant, this is what we'd do."
I passed out again.

The water turned from scalding to temperate, and although I was weak, I no longer passed out. For the last time my mother loomed over me, bringing her face very close to mine. With narrowed eyes and lips pulled taught, enunciating each word clearly, she said, "If you ever tell anyone what happened, I'll kill you." I believed her.

Eventually I became pregnant and had my children, but the anatomic infertility that had prevented pregnancy for so long was diagnosed as being partially due to internal scarring from the burns I received in this incident. I had obeyed my mother's injunction of silence and learned to repress the anguish of my abuse. But the denial of pain ultimately became more than I could bear, and although I descended from repression into the unimaginable terrors of clinical depression, it forced me to seek resolution of my past. When I finally broke the silence, the very utterance of this, and other experiences, shattered the legacy's, and my mother's, hold over me.

Confronting my past presented me with the opportunity to recreate my life with a new vision. My return to college, finding my own voice, and being able to write about my past became possible by prevailing over that past. The most significant evidence of the finality of the legacy's demise are the stories and essays my son creates from his own unencumbered imagination.

TO YOUR BLACK EYES

Now is the part where I tell you that I saw a ghost. And not just any ghost, I saw *her*.

Families have traditions, right? You probably have some in your own. Some families go camping every summer, some fathers coach their kids' baseball team, all that wholesome stuff. Our family had a tradition of seeing shit that in all likelihood wasn't there, telling people about it, and sounding crazy as all fuck. Dad got taken away when we were little because he saw Chinese spies 'monitoring' us in the park outside our place. We were too young to remember the incident, but to hear Mom tell it to me years later she was terrified, and Mom didn't scare easily.

But she had her crazy moments too—always talking about this ghost or that one, and always too casually — a trademark characteristic of people who've slid a little too far down the mental illness rabbit hole. Told me once that she saw her dad in the subway once—ten years after that piece of shit had kindly left this world—said he called her name, she turned towards the sound of the voice, and claimed to have seen his face. When she went over to check, it was some random homeless guy. Never occurred to her that she didn't actually see her dead father, or that telling her son that story in all sincerity was an odd thing to do.

All those qualifications are simply to say this—believe what you want of this story. I'm still not sure what happened, or if it happened at all. All I can tell you is what I remember —the rest is up to you to make sense of.

Right around the whole Russell 2.0 thing, Mom had spiraled back into a deep depression, and any semblance of good days vanished along with her serotonin, leaving yet another round of the Dunbar's favorite family game—(insert game show host voice here) Balance-Those

-Meds! It was a game we never won, like those rigged hook-the-stuffed-animal games at arcades, but just like stupid kids at a birthday party we played nonetheless.

You never quite understand how important one person can be to a family until they're either gone or, in Mom's case, on the sideline. Once she spiraled, holes in our family dynamic got even more exposed. Dad got weird, never really learning how to navigate the waters of Sick Mom with any kind of grace. Instead of becoming a better father, he just kind of became an overly cheery in-home nurse, and one who still worked a full-time job, leaving the vast majority of Mom tasks to me and Clover.

It was at times like those that I normally leaned on my friends, but my latest and greatest had decided to take Russell back, so needless to say I was spending a lot of time by myself. I played a lot of basketball with Carmine and Damien to pass the time, and I spent a lot of time inside, hanging out in my room and honing my nerdiness to a fine, fine point.

Besides all of that, Clover and I were growing ever more distant. She was into three things at that age—hanging out with Serafina, achieving as much as she could in school, and hating the fact that she was a part of our family. It was the last part that was driving a wedge between the two of us.

When I got mad at her for calling our parents crazy ('you sound just like those bullies at school') or at my dad for just being himself, or at the universe for dealing my mom such a shitty hand in life, I'd retreat to the solitude of my room and hang out with Spider-Man, Wolverine, and Jean Grey. They were my second family. And it was then, when I was alone and really sad, that Angela came to me.

I'd always wondered what it would be like to live in a haunted house, and I used to say as much whenever I had the chance.

"What do you think ghosts really do?" I'd ask my sister.

"What do you mean 'really do'?"

"There are a million haunted house books and movies—do you think that they're real? That ghosts act like that? Moving objects and appearing for seconds to people and then disappearing? Or do you think that's just what sells books and movies?"

"I think you're making a huge assumption in that question."

That was what Clover did sometimes. She avoided questions by questioning the question itself, like a teacher would.

"And what's that?"

"That ghosts exist at all. The rest of your question is silly if we're talking about fictitious things."

"Jesus, Clover, just play along. Who cares if they're real or not? And they are, by the way. But just assume I'm right."

"What if I don't want to?"

"Okay, fine, forget ghosts. Let's just say that if there's a possibility that something could exist—maybe a type of animal or something—would it behave like people imagine it would behave, or do you think it would be totally different than what people imagined it to be?"

That's what you had to do with my sister—reframe the questions you wanted to ask her until it was in a form that she felt comfortable answering. She actually wasn't trying to be difficult most times, she was just so far in her head that she needed to make sense of things before she could treat them seriously.

"I think, in that case, that whatever it was would act in whatever way it was capable of, not necessarily in the ways that people's minds could make up."

I found out the answer to my question, and when I did it was nothing like in the movies. No moving chairs. No screaming. No talking pig heads. It was calm. It was peaceful, and this is how it happened.

I'd had another fight with Dad over something stupid that I probably overreacted to. I had a tendency to do that with him, but I had my reasons. Or at the very least I had my teenaged justifications. Before we were born, Dad was a real piece of shit. That sounds harsh to say, but there's no way around it. Another bad man in a family of bad men, only this one was the guy who created me. I'd heard about all of his past indiscretions—the countless infidelities, the drugs, the booze, the verbal abuse, all of it. I'd never agree with Clover to her face, but she was right about one thing—I was probably too young to know those things about my father. Maybe I never should have known. Maybe some things in a marriage are meant to be kept secret, the fine print of the wedding vows that reads 'we promise to not tell our children about the people we really are.'

But Mom did tell me, in some detail, and I never looked at him the same way after that. Ironic, because he'd made an honest attempt to turn himself around and be a better person, but all I could see was the man he used to be before I even existed, and I treated him accordingly.

So after another random fight about another random thing, I ended the night up in my room, alone. I'd stayed up stewing in my own juices as long as I could, rereading as many Spectacular Spider-Man comics as my eyeballs could handle before eventually passing out on my bed. I'm not sure what woke me, but my eyes popped open in the middle of the night. I didn't see anything at first, but once I sat up and cleared my eyes I saw my great grandmother sitting there, as real as the beating of my heart.

I knew it was her because she looked just like she did in the photos I'd seen after Mom told me her story. She had jet black hair, and her face was angelic. At first, I was freaked out, but I didn't think to scream, and it didn't occur to me to run away or call for help. I did what people do in movies when they see something fantastical—I rubbed my eyes again to make sure I wasn't dreaming. When I removed my hands she was still there, even more apparent than before.

Not only was she still there, but she was in even clearer focus than she had been. I didn't move—didn't speak, just looked on with awe. And then she extended her hand in my direction. Part of me thought I was hallucinating, and the other part was so deeply terrified that I just let my body carry me through the motions of what happened next. If I'd stopped to think—really think—about what was happening, I would have cried out, or ran out of the room, or yelled for someone to come see what I was seeing. But I didn't do any of that. All I did was what I was supposed to do—I reached out with my own hand, and committed my trembling flesh to my dead great grandmother's touch.

It's hard to describe what happened next, but the best way to describe it is to say that I lost myself—I ceased to exist as I knew myself to exist. I had no body, no breath, and no voice, only the facility to see whatever I was meant to see, without context or explanation as to what was happening. For whatever reason I didn't panic, but rather submitted to the events that unfolded, even though I struggle, still, to explain them in an accurate way.

The first time Angela took my hand I was still next to her, only we weren't in my room any longer. She was young, very young, beautiful, and sitting poised over an outstretched piece of paper, holding a pen. She struggled with what to write, putting pen to paper, then removing it, several times over, each time her face growing more and more frustrated.

She seemed. . . lonely. The room was unknown to me, but didn't look like anything I'd see in my life. It was large, spacious, and the unmistakable smell of the sea flooded the room through open windows. When at last she picked up the pen again, she committed to the thoughts she'd been laboring over, and I stood behind her as she wrote these words:

Remember,
Even if you cross rivers and seas,
Even if you become a king
Where ever you live
Never forget your wife Angelikh,
My dearest Thanasi,
May you be healthy and happy,
And always have my name in your mind,
And never forget your lonely wife.
Sweet kisses to your black eyes.
Your wife,
Angelikh A. Spuropoulou
September 8th, 1914

And then I was gone again, away from Angela, somewhere decidedly more familiar. I still couldn't speak, and I suspected that I had no form for the people walking the crowded streets to see. I just watched, as people moved about these city streets like ants, speaking more languages than I'd ever heard before.

I'm not sure how long I was there, but eventually one man drew my attention more than the others. He was walking just like everyone else, yet he was dressed impeccably compared to all the other men around him, and his face was adorned with a mustache that ran the length of his lips before curling slightly upwards near each of his cheeks. He looked distinguished, confident, like a man who ill belonged in that part of town.

As he walked, I followed, tracking him from behind like a shadow. When at last he stopped it was by an alleyway in a part of town where there were few people. The people who were around were women, scantily dressed, standing in groups around the side of this building. I couldn't hear the words exchanged, but the man in the suit with the mustache reached into his billfold and gave the woman a sum of money before they both disappeared into the darkness of the alley.

That's when I woke up, alone in my room, confused as I've ever been, the smell of sulfur barely perceptible.

NO SUCH THING AS CRAZY

That happened on a Friday. On Saturday morning I was woken up by our dad knocking on my door, telling me that I had a visitor.

"It's Saturday morning, who could it possibly be?" I asked.

"It's Fina. She's waiting downstairs. Mom's entertaining her."

Almost everything seemed to be wrong with that sentence. First, Fina had barely spoken to me because she was lost in New Boyfriend world; the fact that she was calling on me at the wee hours on a random Saturday seemed weird, and the idea of Mom chatting it up with her this early was the icing on the crazy cake.

"Really? What time is it?" I asked.

"It's just about eight."

"Jesus. Alright, tell her I'll be down in a. . ."

That's when I saw her, standing in my doorway, looking like a heart that had shattered into so many pieces—like that glass Dad broke in the sink last year. He'd ripped his whole hand open and I had to go with him to urgent care after

147

dinner. They stitched him up, but for a while he had gnarly looking scars all over his hand. That's what Serafina's expression reminded me of. I wasn't the most perceptive kid in the world, but I understood the face of sorrow like I understood that with great power came great responsibility. That face was unmistakable—it didn't matter who wore it, it remained a mask that could replace any normal expression. I knew it well.

"Hey," she said softly, standing in my doorway.

"Hey. I haven't seen you in a while."

"I know," she said, sounding almost apologetic. "I'm sorry. I've been a little lost. I get lost sometimes."

"What do you mean?"

"It's just a word I use for feelings I don't like. I get lost sometimes."

I didn't know what she was specifically talking about, but I understood her tone. "Are you still. . . lost?"

"Kinda. I think so. I'm not so sure how to tell the difference between lost and found anymore. Maybe that's why I'm here."

"To be found?" I asked.

"I don't even know, Nate. I just wanted to see you is all. I missed you."

Those words I understood perfectly, and it was music to my ears. "I missed you too. A lot. What happened? Why'd you ditch all of us for. . . why'd you ditch us?"

"I don't know. When I'm lost I'm not myself. I make dumb decisions. I snap at the people I love. And the worst part is when I'm like that, it's like I can't even listen to reason. I don't care what anyone has to say. It's hard to explain."

"You're doing good. I'm not sure what to say back to you, but I understand what you're saying."

"I'm sorry is what I'm trying to say, Nate. I don't know how good of a job I'm doing, but I am sorry for how I treated you and Clover. I wasn't trying to be mean or rude to any of you."

The truth was my anger at her was really just worry I didn't know how to express. I worried about her choice in guys, I worried about her family life, basically I just worried —and never more than the weeks before she walked into my room at eight in the morning to tell me that she was lost.

"It's okay. I don't want you to be lost. You're found whenever you're here."

She walked over and put her arms around me. It wasn't just a hug, it was the mother of hugs—a squeeze that I wanted to disappear into. I didn't ask what she'd done during the time I barely saw her, and I didn't ask about Russell. He didn't matter at that moment. All that mattered was that I had my friend back.

I was so stuck in that moment that I forgot what had happened last night, or at least what I thought happened. As she practically squeezed the life out of me I knew that I needed to tell her. I didn't even know what I was going to say, or how crazy the story would seem, but I knew I had to do it. She let go of me eventually, and our faces reversed.

"What's the matter? Usually a hug doesn't make people look so sad."

"It's not the hug," I told her. "The hug was epic."

"What then?"

"I've been. . . going through some shit. I don't know how to explain it exactly."

"With your mom?"

"Why do you ask that?"

"I don't know, I didn't mean anything by it. She just seemed a little fragile when we talked. More than last time."

There was my Serafina—perceptive as ever. "She's having a rough time, but that's not what I mean. That's always there. This was something else."

"What? You can tell me, Nate, I won't judge you. Listening is the least I can do after all you've put up with."

She sat down on the side of my bed next to me, her weight sinking the mattress slightly, and then she reached out and placed her hand over mine. For a second, I could feel her heart beating. She looked over at me with nothing but a willingness to listen. She didn't want to talk, or to interpret, or analyze. She was just waiting for my words, so that's what I offered.

"I saw my dead great-grandmother last night. She was sitting right over there."

Her next words remain some of the most unexpected of my life.

"What did she say?" I searched her face for any hint of humor or sarcasm, but they weren't there. She really believed me. I don't know how long I stared at her without speaking, but it felt like an eternity. That's when I told her the story— all of it, exactly as I remembered. When I was finished I looked down at the floor, because the floor wouldn't look back. The floor never judged me, it just listened.

"Were you afraid?"

"I was a little startled at first, but not really, no. Maybe I should be scared that I wasn't scared. I think that's because she felt really. . . familiar. I don't know if that makes sense, since I never met her, but I wasn't worried at all."

"Well then you didn't see the ghost of your great grandmother, Nate. You just saw your great grandmother."

Sometimes feelings are impossible to articulate. No words can do them justice. That was one of those moments. I can't tell you the how or the why, but all I could think was how beautiful she was. Not just her face, but everything. Her face, her energy, her vulnerability, all of it just flooded me with feelings of love that I'd never known before. It was instantaneous, like a scene in a movie, and at that moment I loved Serafina more than anything that I'd ever loved before —in ways I didn't need to define for anyone.

"Thank you for saying that."

"You don't have to thank me," she answered. "There are things in this world that we can't explain. They happen all the time, but people are too afraid to talk about them. Too afraid to talk about a lot of things that matter." She trailed off during the last part, her voice fading with each word, until it trailed off almost entirely, her words following her eyes to the ground.

"Yeah," I said to break the silence. "I guess that's true. I was just worried that I was going crazy like my mom."

"There's no such thing as crazy, Nate. There never was. That's a word people invented so that they could dismiss people who said and did things that are 'unacceptable'. But there's no such thing—it isn't real. You saw what you saw, and it was as real as you need it to be."

As real as I needed it to be. That part stuck with me for years, and after she listened to me I felt a little less crazy. "Are you leaving now?" I asked.

"I've gotta go get back home. I just needed to get out for a few. Have you told anyone else about your experience?"

"No," I said. "I didn't, and I don't really plan to, either."

"So then why did you tell me?"

I thought for a second, not sure what to say but needing to say something. "Because this is the kind of thing you tell someone special, who you trust, and you're both." She smiled like she was unaccustomed to being told anything good about herself. But I meant every word of what I said.

"Thank you for trusting me."

"Of course I trust you," I told her. "And hey, can we get back to being normal? Like, you and me normal?"

"Well it's not like I'll be hanging around Russell anytime soon."

That was all I needed to hear. It wasn't a prerequisite for everything that happened, but it secretly made me happy that she'd come to her senses, at least for the time being.

"Oh," I said coyly. "I'm sorry."

"Come on, you hated him."

"Hate," I corrected her. "Present tense."

"I get it. You were just looking out for me. I'm sorry I couldn't hear you. All of you."

"It's okay. Come here." I opened my arms as wide as I could, and when she came close I wrapped them around her. As soon as I squeezed she pulled back and winced. "What's the matter? Did I hurt you?"

"No," she said, grabbing her arm. "It's not you. I'm just. . . a little sore right there."

"Your arm?"

"Yeah, sorry to pull away."

"It's alright." We hugged again, only this time I didn't touch her arm or squeeze very hard, but my spidey sense was tingling something awful. Something was wrong, but I didn't know what, and she wasn't saying. "Remember when I said that I trusted you?" I asked.

"Yeah."

"Can you tell me what happened to your arm?"

My question hung in the air for what seemed like forever, and I watched her intently in the ensuing silence. She did all sorts of subtle things, each of them meant to figure out how to address what I'd just asked. She looked around, breathed deeply, fidgeted a little, then looked back at me with eyes that seemed to be asking me to drop the issue. But I wanted to know what was going on.

"It's nothing, Nate. Please don't ask me again. I hurt it, alright. It's no big deal. I've gotta go."

"Wait, hold on."

"I'll call you later. Tell Clover sorry for me."

"Fina?" I called. She turned back around, but only for a second, only long enough to say one thing.

"Happy early birthday, Nate."

Before I could call her again she was halfway out of my house. She moved fast, her feet carrying her away with purpose, even though I didn't know exactly what that purpose was. But I had my suspicions. I sat on my bed for a few minutes, thinking about everything that had happened in the past twelve hours. My head wouldn't stop spinning, and I would have been hard pressed to name the emotions that I was feeling—some weird hybrid between happy, sad, relieved, and really confused. Whatever that was called, that's what I was feeling.

My birthday—excuse me—*our* birthday was a week later. But I didn't feel celebratory, I felt bewildered by whatever had just happened. I must have been sitting there a while, lost in thought, because it was Clover who snapped me out of it when she opened the door to my room with a gentle knock. "Nate? Can I come in?" The sound startled me at first, but as soon as I saw my sister's face I came back to reality. There were no ghosts of dead relatives, no girls whose relationship with me was too complicated to define properly—there was just the strangely comforting sight of my sister's face. "What's wrong?"

"What do you mean?" I asked. She could always read me like an open book.

"Your face is weird."

"Gee, thanks," I joked.

"No," she said. "Not like that. I meant your expression. Everything okay?"

I ignored her question because I had no way of answering it truthfully, and I wasn't even sure what the truth was. "Did you see Fina before she left?"

"Fina was here?"

"Yeah," I answered. "A few minutes ago. Right where you're standing."

"That's weird that she didn't come to see me. What did she want?"

"She wanted me to tell you that she's sorry for all that shit with Russell. I got the impression that's over. And we just talked."

"She came here so early just to apologize? I don't know what's going on with her lately."

"It's funny you say that."

"How come?" she asked.

"She was hurt," I said. "Her arm. I went to give her a hug and she pulled away. She was hurt and she wouldn't say why. When I asked she got strange and ran off."

"Huh," Clover said. "I wonder why."

"I think I know why." The anger in me was rising, and I knew that the expression on my face had gone from weird to pissed off. "I think I know exactly what happened."

"Relax, Nate, you look so. . ."

"Russell," I said before she could finish. "I know he hurt her."

THE SPINNING BACK FIST
INCIDENT

A week passed at school. Despite her apology Fina was distant from everyone. I saw her in the hall, waved and smiled, but she seemed stuck in her own head. Every time I laid eyes on her I reflected back on the morning she came over to apologize.

I'd convinced myself that I knew what was going on. It was as simple as connecting what were, to me, the obvious dots. Russell was a bad guy, he was dating my friend, they broke up, and now she had this mysterious thing with her arm. It was simple. Russell must have grabbed her, or hurt her somehow, and Serafina didn't want me to do anything about it. My logic wasn't just confirmation bias at work. Russell had a history with that sort of thing, and that history's name was Teresa.

Teresa Kazinski was Russell's first high school girlfriend that anyone knew of. He was older than us, so we were still in middle school when this whole incident happened. But whatever the events of that day actually were, the story I'm about to tell you became infamous.

The story goes that after about two months of dating in

their sophomore year, Teresa and Russell broke it off. According to Russell, he dumped her because she 'wasn't that hot anyway', but according to Teresa, it was because Russell's jealousy was on another level. By her account, Russell got jealous of her best friend, a kid named Teddy Robertson, whom she'd known since they were little. Apparently having a male best friend wasn't a thing when you were Russell's girlfriend, and he started accusing her of cheating. When she tried to break it off he grabbed her and threw her to the ground. She tripped on a rock and twisted her ankle.

By the time the cops arrived at Russell's house to question him for Teresa's assault she was nice and bruised up, not only from the fall (people said her ankle was twice its normal size), but her arms were red and sore. I don't know what came of the legal side of it, and I didn't really care. All I could think was that this seemed just like that. Impressionable girl, check. Male best friend to be jealous of, check. Abusive piece of shit, double check. It all fit, and I was prepared to do something about it. I made my plan one day after school. Clover, being Clover, tried to stop me.

"Nate, getting arrested for beating up Russell isn't the answer."

"They don't arrest kids, Clover. You're watching too much TV."

"We're not little kids, Nate. If you hurt him—like, really hurt him, then you can get arrested, or Mom and Dad can get in trouble. That's the last thing this family needs."

I understood what my sister was saying. It made sense. It was logical. It was correct. But I didn't care. I was still seeing red. I didn't answer her, I just walked downstairs and grabbed the house phone to dial Carmine—I knew he'd be with me no matter what. I'd told him about my plan at school, and he was ready for action when I needed him to be.

I knew Russell would be at Jared's house—they always hung out there in the evening because Jared's parents worked late shifts at their jobs. He lived a few duplexes down from us, and as far back as I could remember he'd always been a degenerate. He was half a high school career older than us, and he and Russell were birds of a feather. We could see his bedroom window from our living room, and it became our favorite spectator sport. A bag of popcorn was required for every viewing of the crazy shit happening a few feet above his parents' noses.

We'd watch random skanks sneaking out his window at all hours. We'd watch him lean out to smoke copious amounts of weed right in broad daylight. Kid had no shame, and at school it was even worse. At school those kinds of things made him cool, made him the one who had stories to wow the less experienced kids with. At school his buffoonery made him King Shit.

"You alright, man?" I overheard Russell ask him in the hallways one day.

"No fuckin' brain cells left, dude. Zero."

"Man, you gotta go easy."

"Screw easy," Jared said, barely able to string a sentence together. "I've never been so messed up before. It was awesome."

That was Jared. Stupid and proud of it. Today they'd call him an 'at risk' youth, but back then he was just your run of the mill piece of shit that every neighborhood came standard with. He had parents, but they'd given up any hope of trying to change who their son was. His mom was a nice lady who never missed a chance to say hello to us kids and ask how our day was. That's about as much as any of us knew about her—

that she was the nice mom of a shitty human being. But something had clearly gone wrong in that home, and I can't help but think some of that had to have been on her. Jared's dad was nice enough on the surface—always a wave and a hello—but he was angry all the time, and didn't seem to make much of an attempt to hide it from anyone. Their duplex was close enough to ours that we could hear the screaming, which was frequent and loud. It happened a few times a week, at least.

"I'm going over there," I reiterated to Clover.

"Why? How are you so sure you know that he had something to do with her being hurt?"

It was a valid question, and one that I should have listened to in hindsight, but I didn't. I was too busy playing the hero. Clover jumped in to try to be the voice of reason, like she so often did, but I wasn't in the mood to listen to reason. "Nathan, he's just the asshole down the street. He didn't do anything."

"We'll see."

Carmine rang our doorbell five minutes later. In the interim I'd changed out of a nice shirt into one fit for a fight (that old tee we all keep in our closets in case we need to throw down), gotten even more angry at the whole situation, and was ready to throw hands by the time I left. Even though my bestest wasn't really the fighting type, two on two was better than two on one any day. Carmine was a good solider —he didn't ask many questions in situations like this, he'd just back me up. I went to answer the door as Clover tried to convince me one more time to not do what I was about to do, but her words fell on deaf ears. I opened the front door to the sight of my best friend, ready for war.

"Let's do this shit," he said.

"Amen, brother."

"What are we doing exactly?"

I smiled even though what I was feeling was anything but funny. "I'll tell you later. Right now, I just need a wingman."

"I'm your guy. Let's go."

We marched over to Jared's house. I was so sure that Russell would be there that I didn't even check first. Like I said before, the Meadows was a small place in a lot of ways, and not only did we know each other's gossip, we knew the comings and goings of everyone in the neighborhood. Both of Jared's parents worked evenings, so I knew he'd be in the house alone. Well, almost alone.

"Hey asshole," I yelled. "Come and get some. It's time."

Jared opened his window and I could see the puff of smoke. Behind that haze I saw them both, grinning like morons, already high as kites. "What? Who's there?"

"It's Nate. We gotta talk, Russell, you and me. Now come down here."

Carmine just stood behind me like some kind of enforcer, never saying a word but doing his best to look tough. He was a big kid, so even though he wasn't really a fighter his size worked to his advantage. Russell and Jared looked at each other and smiled, and I felt the rage rising in my throat. I saw them back away from their window and I knew they were on their way down. Jared's back door opened a minute later, and my heart started racing.

The reason Clover was so worried was because she knew what I was capable of. We were in the same high school now, and we'd been in the same school for 8th grade, but for a year prior to that I went to a private school. The reason for my almost year long sabbatical from public school was because of a kid named Eric Graftson. Eric and I knew each other from around, but he lived far enough away that I only ever saw him at school, or occasionally at a random basketball court in the neighborhood. We never got along. Oil and water.

We just kind of tolerated each other, and we would have remained nothing more than two ships in the junior high night, except for the fact that he was always mean to my sister. Nothing so overt—more of a death by a thousand paper cuts kind of bullying. Eventually in the 7th grade I reached a breaking point. They never put Clover and I in the same classes—some shit about twins needing their own identities. But as the scheduling gods had it, Eric and her were in a lot of the same 7th grade classes. One day, right around Thanksgiving, she came out of school red eyed and visibly upset. Eric had been torturing her all day about about how she looked, about our parents, about all sorts of things.

Eric and I didn't share many classes, but as fate would have it, we had the same lunch period. I went up to him in the cafeteria the next day and tapped him on the shoulder as he sat with his friends. "Did you make fun of my sister?" I asked. He stood up, a few inches taller than me, and out weighing me by at least twenty pounds. He thought his size advantage was a real thing, that I'd back off when he puffed his chest out. He didn't really know me.

"Yeah. What of it?"

It might sound strange, but I told him that I was about to hit him. He laughed hysterically, like he thought I was joking. The way I saw it, even though starting a fight wasn't the best thing to do, I wasn't about to sucker punch the kid. So I let him know what was about to happen in good faith. It was up to him to defend himself. What happened next is still a blur all these years later. I know that they pulled me off of him and there was blood all over me —Eric's blood—and I remember him being on the ground, and the sound of frenzied yelling all around. The next real memory I have was when my parents came to get me, a superintendent's hearing where I was suspended indefinitely, and a lot of yelling at home. It took months of negotiating before the school would agree to let me back for my last year of middle school. Eric avoided me like the plague.

I felt that way again on the morning of the Spinning Back Fist From Hell. I was older, a little more mature, but I still had that dangerous thing inside of me that came out in moments like this—moments where I had to defend those who couldn't defend themselves.

"What do you want, man?"

"I want to talk about Serafina."

He and Jared startled giggling. I could smell the weed on them and it almost made me gag. "What's funny?"

"I kicked that bitch to the curb. What, you like her or something?"

"I'm not here to talk about that. I want to know what you did to her?"

"What do you mean?"

"Cut the shit. I know you hurt her just like you hurt Teresa."

I knew I'd hit a nerve if I brought her up, and when I invoked his first victim's name his face contorted—his smile disappeared and was replaced by shock and anger.

"What did you say, you little shit?"

"I know you like to hurt girls, but what about guys? You too afraid to fight one of them."

"Keep talking, dick, and I'll show you how not afraid I am."

That was all I needed to hear. But this time I couldn't be the instigator. I couldn't throw the first punch. I learned from 7th grade that once you do that all sympathy is gone, and you're the guilty party no matter what. I needed him to throw first.

"How about this? Maybe I'll go to your house first, find your mom, and throw her down like you threw Teresa down. How about that?"

There was a cardinal rule with guys—never invoke each other's mom's names in a negative way. There were some exceptions. You could joke around with good friends sometimes, but it was a limited thing. But with people you barely knew or, even better, people you didn't like, it was a taboo—fighting words.

He did what I knew he'd do. He stepped forward and swung at me with a looping right hand. I took a small step back, enough to feel the wind generated by his punch as it missed my face, and as I did I started to spin. Dad was a martial artist—he used to train people in the neighborhood for free, and I'd get left alone because everyone assumed that the kid of a martial artist had to be tough. I wasn't that tough, but I had learned enough for situations like that. The spin probably lasted a nanosecond, but, once my fist hit his face he was taken off his feet by the momentum, and landed on the ground, conscious but stunned.

I waited for him to get up, ready to fight if I had to, but he didn't. Jared tried to step towards me but Carmine, my soldier, matched his forward advance, stopping Jared dead in his tracks. He backed up and attended to his friend, whose face looked like a red Crayola crayon. He got up, but I could see right away he had no interest in fighting. He was scared.

"You're fucking psycho, just like your parents."

I stepped forward, but Carmine grabbed me. "Stop, man. You made your point."

As Russell and Jared retreated back into Jared's house my heart continued to pound in my chest. And just like that, it was over. But I didn't feel any better. In fact, I felt worse. Despite the fact that he deserved to get hit, I felt bad for losing control like I did.

The rest of the day passed without incident. I remember thinking that the cops were going to show up at my house to arrest me for assault, and how that might affect Mom's state of mind. But it never happened. Later on that evening I tried calling Serafina. I got Damien instead.

"She's out," he told me. "Said she went for a walk or something, I'm not sure."

"Okay. Well tell her I called, okay."

"You got it, man."

I wanted her to walk to my house, to tell her that I'd defended her honor and fucked up that piece of crap. But it never happened like that. No one came to the house—not the cops, not Fina, no one. The night ended like most of my nights ended—with me reading a comic, wondering what exactly had become of my life.

MY HEART BURNS THERE TOO

You've probably seen this moment coming, haven't you? You were just too polite to say anything. I mean, with all my declarations earlier you must have at least suspected that at some point my platonic love for Serafina would turn into actual love. The platonic part was true enough, at least in the beginning, but the more time passed and longer we spent in each other's company the more my feelings towards her changed into something much deeper.

I fought it at first—rejected the idea outright, to the point of complete denial. *No, stupid, you're not in love with Fina, you're just confused because you're really protective of her and she's beautiful, that's all.* Just your standard teenaged confusion, I told myself, nothing more or less. But the more I shoveled my own bullshit the harder it became to ignore the smell. Eventually I had no choice but to give in and admit how I felt. The realization scared and excited me, and I had no good idea what to actually do with all those feelings I was bottling up inside. They built and built until finally I broke, and I knew that I had to tell her.

I know what you're thinking—good old Nate's got a

messed up best friend, two crazy parents, and a bunch of normal teenaged shit to deal with, why add to that pile by risking rejection from a girl? Wouldn't that just add a nice layer of Cool Whip to the shit sandwich that was life at the time? Probably, but the feelings themselves didn't make sense, why should my actions be any different. I had to tell her, the question was just how and when.

What I realized is that the whole thing with Russell and Fina lit a flame under my ass. If I'm being honest with myself it wasn't just some misguided sense of protection I felt when that whole thing took place, it was also a fair amount of jealousy. What the whole thing taught me was that if I didn't risk telling her how I felt, no matter the consequences that ensued, there would be plenty of guys who would. Maybe not guys exactly like Russell, but there would surely be a small army of others before we graduated high school. Serafina would still be my friend, and we'd still be cool, but sooner or later some dude would come along and take her from me in a way that was more permanent than I was willing to accept. So my decision was made, I decided to tell her. Sort of.

Tell her makes it sound like I was going to make some grand gesture like John Cusack in *Say Anything*, but there was no way that was going to happen. Instead I did what I'd later make my career in life doing—what I'm doing right now —I wrote.

I should've known that I was going to be a writer one day. I had all the symptoms, I just lacked the formal diagnosis. I wrote all the time, but not only did I write, I edited, I revised, I stressed over anything that had my name at the top of the page and words underneath, even school assignments that the other kids cheated on or didn't do. It wasn't that I loved homework, and I sure as hell didn't like school, but I wanted to be proud of anything that I created.

So imagine the beads of sweat that formed on my head while writing this letter—this declaration of love. Water works. Needed several showers during the process, and to top it off I had to hide my notebook whenever Clover came in the room. One time she almost caught me.

"What are you hiding?"

"Nothing. What are you talking about?" She gave me the skeptical eyebrows, which I very much deserved.

"Riiight," she joked. "It's fine, keep your secrets."

I decided to double down—the last resort of all bad liars. "No, seriously, for real. I'm just. . . doing homework."

Two mistakes in a row there. One, never hesitate when covering up a lie. Two, never add phrases like 'for real', because they come across as meaning the opposite. Clover took pity on my obvious stretching of the truth—either she respected my privacy or she didn't really care that much about what I was doing in the first place. Either was fine with me, so I didn't press the matter any further when she said, "Alright, I'll leave you alone to your 'nothing' then."

"Okay, thanks. It's really nothing." I don't know why I threw that last part in, I was good.

"Yeah, you said that a few times already."

When she left, I got back to my writing. Mom always read Stephen King. He was like my second dad. His name was always on her lips, and his latest gigantic horror book was always around. I'm not sure why—maybe it was the size of the book—but I'd gotten into reading *It* because I was nerdy like that and I had no qualms about attacking a thousand-page book about a killer clown.

There was a character in *It*—Ben Hanscom. He was the fat kid who was secretly in love with the only girl in 'The Loser's Club', Beverly Marsh. There's a part in the story where Ben decides to leave Beverly a note confessing how he feels about her. I still remember the words without having to check the book:

Your Hair is Winter Fire
January Embers
My Heart Burns There Too

I tried my hand at something short and romantic for Serafina —just a few lines that could express how I felt about her, but it was complete trash. So what did I do instead? I did the opposite of old Ben Hanscom's poem—I wrote her a letter, and a long one at that. Mom and Clover thought something was wrong because I didn't come down for dinner that night. I told them I had a stomach ache, but the real ache was dead center in my chest—and the only way to get it to be even a little bit better was to write.

Now here's the kicker. I didn't sign it. I left it anonymous because I was scared—something I regretted as soon as I dropped it off. I knew that Fina was the first one into her house to get home after school. Hank worked late most nights and, according to Damien, drank even later. Speaking of my friend, I knew he'd be at school for extra help because he was failing five of his seven classes. That left Fina—my favorite latch key kid to open up her house and take in the mail. It was that last part that I was going to exploit. I put my letter in an envelope with her name written in oversized purple letters and left it in the Gilmore's mailbox. We usually walked home together, so despite the fact that I rarely did stuff like this, I cut 9th period so that I could beat her home. I took the letter out of my bag and placed it carefully in front of all of their other mail.

Then, like a true stalker, I waited across the street. I must have looked crazy. Thank God normal people were either at school or work, because I literally crouched behind a big bush in front of one of the Gilmore's neighbor's house directly across the street. I waited and waited until I saw her approaching from down the block. My heart started to pound the closer she got to her mailbox, and I regretted not signing it. Secretly I hoped she'd read it, realize that it was from me, and then come running over to my house and kiss me at the front door. Of course that's not what happened.

Instead I sat on the ground, literally getting my ass dirty with the soil beneath me slowly soaking the bottom of my brand new jeans. My back hurt from the weird position I had to sit in, and I had enough anxiety built up to justify a medicine cabinet's worth of meds. And then I watched her read it, right then and there on her stoop, as I stared from far away, waiting to see some kind of recognition. A smile. A warm smile that would have filled me with hope that maybe —just maybe—she knew it was from me, and that she felt the same way as I did. But there was nothing. No smile. No frown. No anything. She just read it like she was reading the menu of some new Chinese take out place that had been left by a local vendor. When she was done she folded it, put it in her back pocket, and disappeared inside their duplex.

The day after I gave her my letter was my birthday—our birthday—the day Fina disappeared.

I always knew that the two things were related.

TO ERASE EVERYTHING SHE WAS

That night I had a vision.

I'd moped through the rest of the day, feeling weird about the whole letter thing, to the point where even Mom was worried about me. I did my usual 'nothing's wrong' routine, even though something was very wrong, and after dinner I dragged myself up to my room to just chill out, read some comics, and eventually go to sleep, and sleep.

I passed out at some point, but ended up opening my eyes. I'm not sure if I was dreaming or not, or if I was in some strange state in between consciousness and sleep, but once my eyes were open I wasn't in my room anymore. In fact, I wasn't in my house anymore at all. Suddenly I was in a home that wasn't my own, watching a family go about their day as though I were watching a film of their lives. They didn't see me, and I had no form, but I saw and heard everything that was happening within their walls.

I heard the screaming first. A man's voice, gravelly and deep, shouting forceful words I couldn't understand. I saw the children in the home, some of whom were almost grown and some of whom weren't, run towards their front door to hear the grumbling in the hallway of their apartment. The mother tried to stop them, but gave up quickly. The children—there were five of them—rushed the door, and the oldest of them, a girl who looked about twenty, opened it with some force. I still couldn't see the man, but his yelling was clearer now, and with each passing second it grew closer.

The girl stepped into the hallway for a moment and returned minutes later with a man—the same man from last time, with the curled mustache and tan skin, only he was much older now, and disorganized in his appearance. He looked like he'd just woken from a dream as she brought him inside.

"Papa," she cried. "Stop it. You can't do this anymore."

"It's the dog. It's that goddamn dog that keeps pissing in the halls."

"Papa, there's no dog. The halls are empty. There's never been a dog—they're not allowed in this building, it's against the rules."

"Nonsense, I see it every day. It runs away from me when I yell, so I follow it. I'm not about to let a dog outsmart me, but whenever I get close it runs some more. I'm afraid I'll never catch it."

The girl brought her father over and sat him down on their couch. The other kids brought him tea and took his shoes off.

Then the scene changed. Even though I had no body, I felt the cold. I was on a rooftop—their rooftop, as the mother was drying a never-ending basket of clothes. It was freezing up there, and the wind blew hard, throwing the shirts and pants aside with some force. As I watched her do laundry the man approached, and as he did she recoiled in fear.

"What is it?" she asked. "I'm hanging the children's clothes."

"Not again!" he yelled, stepping closer to her in a way

that made her back up. "I know what you've been doing. I know about the men."

"What men?" she asked, the fear in her eyes unmistakable.

"The men you've made a fool of me with. All of them. Too many to count. You thought you could hide them, but I know things. You can't hide what you do from me. I hear the neighbors whispering about it—laughing at me. I won't be made a fool of!"

The woman was confused, and frightened in place. As he spoke he walked her down, and she instinctively backed up, inch by inch, until she was only a foot from the edge of their roof. She looked over her shoulder, down to the cold concrete below, then back to her husband, who hadn't yet relented pushing her ever more backwards.

"Stop it!" she yelled. "There are no men. Stop it."

That's when he grabbed her by the arm, and she yelled where no one could hear. It was clear in that moment that her life wasn't her own—it was his. He owned her and all that she was. He had control over her life and death, over her mind, body and soul, and all it would have taken was an extension of his arms to erase everything she was.

"Next time I catch you, I'm going to kill you. If I see another man leaving here at night, I'm going to bring you back to this roof, and I'm going to push you off of it. Do you understand me?"

Then, just like that, he walked away. The woman collapsed near the edge of the roof and sobbed, uncontrollably, until it was the only sound I could hear. Then it was over. I was back in my room, disoriented at what I'd just seen, the beating of my heart so fast that my chest ached.

THE STRANGEST BIRTHDAY EVER

Say what you will about Dad, but he always made a big deal about our birthdays. I woke up that morning—actually, I was woken up that morning, fresh from whatever dream I had the night before by our dad yelling like it was Christmas morning. His cheer distracted me from the horror of what I'd just seen that night.

"Happy birthdays, babies."

"Jesus, Dad, it's early." My eyes were barely open, my brain still foggy from whatever I'd experienced. "And we're not babies anymore," I said.

"You're right and you're wrong," Dad answered back. "It is early, but you'll always be my babies, no matter how old you are."

"Does every parent use that line at some point?" I asked.

"I think so. And you will, too, one day, trust me."

"I don't know about all that," I told him. "I think it might be one of those things that gets so annoying to hear that I'' never repeat it."

"You think that now," he said. "But just you wait."

He was wearing a corny paper birthday hat str'

head, and he was rocking his custom-made birthday tee that had pictures of me and Clover right after we were born, still wrapped up in those hospital towels every baby in the world gets put in. Mom didn't come into my room. She was where she always was, in bed. It was my job to wake her up if it got too late, even on weekends. I used to think those birthday mornings were stupid. I'd roll my eyes, even though my teenaged apathy never caused Dad's enthusiasm to waiver. But looking back, as we all have to look back, I wished I'd said thank you once or twice.

Clover was just behind Dad, still in her PJ's and trying her best to smile her way through this. She came over to my bed as I sat up and gave me a big hug, our customary birthday greeting.

"Happy B-Day."

"You too."

This was a time before cell phones—just before—so we got our news, good or bad, the old-fashioned way, from other people telling us. The morning of our birthday there was a ring of the doorbell, which was strange because of the time of day alone. "I wonder who that could be," Dad said, his overly enthusiastic grin turning into a puzzled half-smile as he left our room to answer the door.

As Dad went downstairs Clover sat at the end of my bed. "Where's Mom?" I asked.

"She's asleep, Nate," she explained. "She'll be up soon and she'll wish us a happy birthday. You know how she is."

We heard the noise downstairs. The man's voice sounded familiar, and it was loud and panicked. Dad's voice followed. "Kids, come down here right now, please."

"What's going on?" Clover asked.

"I don't know," I told her. "Let's go find out."

When we got downstairs to see what the commotion was

about we saw the Gilmores—sans Serafina—looking a mess and standing in our living room next to my Dad.

"Mr. Gilmore," I said out of habit as soon as our eyes met.

"Kids, Mr. Gilmore is looking for Serafina. She didn't come home. Have you seen her?"

"No," I told him. "I haven't seen her."

It was right after I said that that he broke down—when you're a kid it's weird to see a grown man cry like Hank Gilmore cried that day, and it was all the more strange because Hank seemed like a hardened man, someone not really prone to much emotion at all, except maybe anger.

"Alright, kids, why don't you go back upstairs. Let me talk with Mr. Gilmore a little longer and see if we can get this business sorted out, okay?"

"Yeah, no problem, Dad."

We went back up to our rooms, confused as ever. What had happened? I'd seen Fina yesterday and now she was missing? Of course I couldn't exactly say where I'd seen her —that I creeped outside of their place in the damn bushes, watching her read a secret love note that I'd cut school to leave in their mailbox. Nah, that wasn't going to fly. The truth had to be put on hold. A minute or so after we got upstairs Damien followed.

"Can I come in?" he asked, knocking gently on my door.

"Yeah, man. Of course."

Damien was a sad kid—he was missing all of those things that having a mom gives you, and he was being raised by a hard ass who in no way understood him. Carmine and I gave him shit, but we loved the kid dearly, and if anyone ever messed with him we woul[...] their ass. And he got messed with a lot. H[...] being a high school kid who was obses[...] wrestling, for dressing the way he did, and f[...]

than a little chubby. But that morning he looked sad-sad. My-sister-is-missing sad.

Like all of us, he dealt as best he could—mostly by hanging with Carmine and I because he knew we'd keep him safe. But that was about all that was guaranteed him. Damien was firmly entrenched at the bottom of the high school social hierarchy, and it was easier to scale Everest than to climb up that slippery pyramid.

"What the hell happened?" I asked.

"We don't know. Dad's all messed up. I have no idea where she is. This isn't like her."

"I'm sure she's okay, she likes to take long walks to clear her head."

"She told you about those?" Damien asked.

"Yeah," I answered. "She tells me a lot of things."

Damien paused for a minute, lost in thought. "Dude, my dad's talking about the police and the FBI. Putting out an Amber Alert, whatever that is. He's losing his mind. You should have seen him before we came over here."

"I can imagine," Clover said. "I'm losing it a little bit too. What if something happened to her?"

"That's unlikely," I said. It sounded too definitive—too sure for the complete lack of evidence that I had, yet somehow deep down I just knew this wasn't a foul play kind of situation. "We don't live in the kind of neighborhood where teenagers get kidnapped. We don't have any crime here, come to think of it." It was true. Outside of the urban legend of the woman assaulted in the laundry room, there was almost no crime to speak of where we lived. The likelihood of a kidnapping seemed a little extreme.

"I really hope you're right."

Damien and his dad left about a half hour later, and that should have been a celebration became what was easily the strangest birthday we'd ever had. Eventually Mom woke up on her own, probably after hearing all the noise Dad and Mr. Gilmore were making in the living room.

"Happy birthday, babies!"

"Do you and Dad practice that line together?" I joked.

"I promise we don't."

I don't know if it's unusual to remember specific hugs, but I remember that one. Not because it was the greatest hug in the history of moms and their sons, and not because it was my birthday. I remember it because of how frail she felt. When we were little Clover and I used to talk about how strong Mom was. She used to feel like iron—like she was made of something unbreakable. When Dad worked late Mom would fill in for him and wrestle around with us. Even at five feet tall she always seemed like a giant, and she had this crazy physical strength for someone her size.

That was how we saw her—as Unbreakable Mom. And in so many ways she remained unbroken, but the disease had bent her as far as was possible to bend, and I felt it that morning in her embrace.

"I believe you," I joked. "But we're not babies anymore."

"You know. . ."

"That we'll always be your babies? We know, Mom, we know."

Dad wanted to talk about what had just happened. "Kids, now that Mr. Gilmore is gone, do you know anything about your friend that you were too afraid to say when he was here? Because he's planning on going to the police, and if this is just some teenaged runaway thing. . ."

"Some teenaged runaway thing?" I repeated. "Jesus, Dad."

"Relax," Clover answered. "He's just trying to help. And

no Dad, there's nothing we didn't tell you. We're just as worried as you are. We don't know where she is."

That was mostly true. From Clover's perspective it was a complete truth, but I knew a little more than she did. The only question was whether or not I should tell her, and whether or not the details of the previous day even mattered.

We did our normal birthday routine after that. Dad made a spread of pancakes, bacon, sausage, and toast, and we scarfed it down like it was our last meal. When we were done, Clover and I excused ourselves and went up to my room to talk.

"It's just you and me now," she said before we'd even closed the door to my room for privacy. "What do you know?"

"What do I know?"

"I thought you might know something. She's been spending a lot of time with you, I thought that maybe you might have a clue as to where she was."

"You really think I have some secret information that I'm not sharing with Dad or Mr. Gilmore, or even you? Hate to break it to you, but I don't."

"Whatever."

"What's your problem? Are you mad she hangs out more with me than with you?"

"I'm mad about a lot of things, Nate. That's just one of them if you want to know the truth."

Clover bottled things up. To use the words that she'd use all the time as an adult once she was in therapy, she 'internalized' and 'suppressed' things a little too much. As an adult that meant one thing, but when we were kids it meant that she kept things to herself until even she couldn't take the feeling of them any longer. Then she'd spew like an uncovered fire hydrant.

"What are you mad about?"

"Do you know what my grades are this marking period, Nate?"

"Your grades?" I asked. "Why are we talking about school right now when Fina. . ."

"Enough about Fina!" she yelled. "It's always about her. I'm struggling like I never have before, Nate. I know you don't feel the same way, but school matters to me. I like doing well. I like working towards goals for the future. And my grades are shit right now. Did you even know that?"

"No," I answered. "How would I know that?"

"And there it is," she said. "How does anyone ever know anything? You ask. Mom and Dad used to always ask about my grades in elementary and even middle school. 'How's science?', or 'Do we need to get you a tutor for math?' They used to sit with me and look at my progress reports and report cards. They used to care, Nate."

"Yeah, I know. They did the same with me. What's your point?"

"My point is that they don't care anymore."

"Mom's sick. Dad's. . . whatever he is. We're getting older. There are other things going on besides your progress reports. I can't believe we're even talking about this right now. I don't get it."

"Yeah," she said. "No one gets it. But let me spell it out for you. Everyone's got a reason to not pay attention to what's going on with me, and all those reasons make sense. Mom's sick, Dad's sick, Fina's missing, you're doing whatever with your friends. But where does that leave me?"

Then Clover did what Clover never did—she started crying. Not angry crying—sad crying, hurt crying. The tears streamed down her face, disarming me completely. I couldn't think to do anything else but hug her.

"Hey, I'm sorry, okay? Don't cry, I didn't realize you were feeling like this."

"No one realizes. No one sees me."

I had a strange thought at that moment that I still remember well enough to write it down now. Clover used to make fun of me for caring so much about our family history. About our great grandmother, about Mom's life before she had us, about all of it. As mature as she could be, she never understood something that I understood fundamentally at a young age—that our past forms our future.

In that instance I thought of Mom, and how she didn't wake up one day depressed, anxious, and barely able to function. She'd had a life, gone to school, gotten married, raised a family, all of it. But I imagined her as a teenager around Clover's age, and how she probably liked school too, only her parents were too supremely fucked up to notice or encourage her. How many times did Mom cry alone in her room before she became like she was? How many people didn't see her for who she really was back then?

"I see you, Clover. I do. I'm so sorry. It's hard for all of us. That's not an excuse, but we all get caught up in our own shit and don't see one another. But I get it now that you told me." She squeezed me back and I gave her my best twin hug. "There we go," I joked. "Gimme the bear hug love!" She giggled, and I felt a little better that I took the edge off of her pain. "Do you wanna like, show me your report card?"

"Why?" she asked. "It would just embarrass you and make you feel bad about yourself."

"There's the Clover I know and love."

"I'm sorry if I'm being selfish."

"Hey, look at me. You're not being selfish, okay? You're not."

"Thanks, Nate. Let's focus on Fina. We can get back to me later on."

"Deal. And like I said I really don't know where she is. I have no idea. But I do know something I didn't say, you were right about that. I just don't know if it matters."

"Tell me."

So I did.

I told her everything, including how I felt about Serafina. Then the note. Then, I waited.

"Well I knew the first part already. I mean, c'mon. It's so obvious."

"What???" Obvious was not the word I would have thought of. I didn't even realize how I felt about Serafina until a little before all of that went down, but I guess Clover did somehow. "Really?"

"Really Nate. Girls know these things. It's in the way you look at her. I always knew, even if it took you a little longer to realize."

"Wow. I don't know what to say."

"Nothing," she answered. "Don't say a word. It's my turn to talk."

"Okay."

"I think I might actually know where she is."

THE MERCHANT OF COFFEE

Clover and I keep walking, sipping our still warm coffees and keeping a brisk pace, until we're at the Oak Grove— a giant, circular piece of land filled with tall trees and a few worn out benches. The Grove sits in the middle of apartment buildings that encircle it on all sides. Today they'd call it a green space —the kind of scenery urban development companies put in so that they can gentrify with impunity. But we had it decades before it became fashionable. It looks the same over here, all these years later. Tall trees. Benches. Peace. A good place to sit and talk.

"What do you know about the. . ."

"The murder?" she asks.

"I was going to say the incident. I don't know why. Force of habit, I guess."

"Yeah. Our family never met a euphemism it didn't like. If we're going to talk about it then we need to call it what it was. Deal?"

"Deal. The murder, then. What do you know about it? Or Angela? Or any of it really."

"I guess I'll answer the last part first. I know that our

great grandmother was named Angela. That she came from Greece with our grandmother, and that she was murdered by her husband when Grandma was very young."

"And?" I ask, searching for any more details that she might know.

"And what? And nothing. That's all I know. That's all I was ever given, Nate. Broad strokes. Am I missing a lot?"

That's a difficult question to answer. We're both missing more than we knew, but the more we speak the more obvious it was to me that Mom kept things from Clover. I don't know if that was because she didn't think my sister could handle the harsh truths she bestowed upon me like I was her confidante, or if she just thought that I could. Either way I was the inadvertent family historian—and, really, I wasn't even that. I didn't have records, or details, or the kinds of evidence that would allow a person to piece together an objective, factual account of the past. All I have is stories, and stories from those who had to live with the remnants of what happened that morning in 1939.

"Everything you said was true. But how much do you know about the murder? Like, the details?"

"Not much. Just that he shot her. I remember Mom saying that once."

"Did you know our grandmother saw the whole thing? That she had to wrestle the gun out of her father's hand so that he wouldn't kill her and the other kids? That she was left alone to raise her siblings?"

"Jesus," she says, her mouth opening ever wider in a look of shock. "Really?"

"Just like I described. At least, that's the best we can know of it with the evidence we have."

"Evidence?" she asks. "You sound like a detective."

I smile. "That's what I've felt like doing this. Even before

this book I was serializing my next one for *The New Yorker*—
that was. . . excuse me, that is going to appear over the next
few months, and it was just going to be an almost true crime
retelling of the murder and its aftermath. I had to become like
a detective. You wouldn't believe how far I had to dig to even
find the smallest amount of public records."

I can see I've peaked her interest. She seems to be
hanging on my words. It's funny to see that expression on her
face because whenever I brought up any family stuff in the
past I got an eye roll and a total lack of interest. But now she
seems engaged in everything I'm saying. "What did
you find?"

"Nothing much, like I said. It was so long ago that you'd
actually have to be a detective or historian to dig up much,
and even then, there's probably not a lot of valid information
about an immigrant apartment complex in 1939 that's not
even there any more. I was lucky to find what I found."

"Which was? You still haven't told me."

"Oh, let me show you."

"Wait, you have with you?"

"On my phone. Look."

I show her the two short articles that I found. Both are
from the New York Times shortly after the murder. The first
is dated the next day—July 23rd, 1939—and the other is dated
two weeks later. I show her original article detailing the
murder. And when I say article, I mean a short paragraph
that's filled with misspelled names, and a shocking casual
treatment of a man who just killed his wife and attempted to
kill his children. It referred to him only as a '. . .coffee
merchant. . .', and told the story of his burgeoning psychosis,
and his final attempt to murder his family. The next one
details his sentencing, along with another local murderer.
Thomas was sent to a psychotic hospital whose records I

couldn't get a hold of. He died there a few years after the murder, and I'm guessing he was buried on premises, or in an unmarked grave for the indigent.

I let Clover read over them quickly before she hands me my phone back. "God, no wonder we're all so fucked up."

"Speak for yourself, Sis."

"No, I'm serious. We're functionally fucked up—like those people who are full fledged drunks but can still somehow hold down jobs and lives. We're the mental health equivalent of those people. And our parents just barely scraped by."

"Well, isn't that good news, then?" I ask.

"How is that good news?"

"Well, look at the pattern you just described. It means that each generation is getting better. That means that our children —and they're the only ones who matter—should be free of all this."

"It's not a debt, Nate. We don't pay it off over a term. Doesn't work that way. We have to earn our health."

"And your solution is therapy and meds you don't like to talk about?" She looks shocked when I say that. We've never discussed the pill bottle incident since it happened, but now seems as good a time as any. "If you don't want to head down the same road as Mom then you need to confront the past, Clover. Not dope yourself up for the rest of your life."

"Fuck you, Nate. I don't need this."

She jumps up and starts walking away from me. To say that I've hit a nerve would be the understatement of the century. I hit more than a nerve—I struck the black gold of our family history, and that's something Clover has never wanted to deal with.

"Stop being dramatic, come back."

She waves her hand, never turning around, and just keeps

on walking. I feel like shit, even though I meant every word that I said. I knew this book might drive a wedge between us, but I didn't know that even talking about this stuff would make her so angry. Before too long she's out of sight. I feel like I just fucked up, big time. What I meant to be a nice afternoon with my sister just turned into an ugly confrontation. I call the only person who can help me in this situation—my wife. I miss her right now.

"Hey there," I say after she picks up on the second ring. "How are you feeling?"

"Very pregnant, Nathan. Like there's a small child living inside of me. Oh, wait!"

"I know, I'm sure you can't wait to just get on with it already."

"Having the baby, yes. The pushing her out of me part? Not so much. But this isn't news. How's everything with your sister going?"

"Well, let's see. She just stormed off in anger after I told her she needs to stop popping psych meds or she'll end up like our mom did."

"Oh, shit. Did you really say that?"

"Uh-huh. Good job, Nate, right? What a shit show."

"Well get off the phone with me and go apologize. Text her then catch up to her. She could't have gone that far."

"People can go really far in this neighborhood on foot— farther than you'd think. You know that already."

"You're batting 1,000 today. What's the matter?"

I take a deep breath and exhale loudly. This day just took a real turn for the worse, and I start to feel like shit about my book. "I'm sorry. I'm just so sick of the bullshit. So sick of the secrecy. All of it. How hard is it to just look the past in the eye and deal with it?"

"You're asking me, of all people?"

"I guess it's rhetorical, but it's a serious question."

"Then let me give you a serious answer before you go find Clover. For some people it's really hard—damn near impossible. Not everyone is comfortable in discomfort like you, Nate, and I mean that as a compliment. But you can't judge everyone who isn't you. It's a sensitive topic—not just your family in general, but her meds. Clover's old enough that she's starting to see your mom when she looks in the mirror. She feels her every time she washes one of those pills down her throat. You're poking an open wound, even if it's decades old."

"I never thought of it that way."

"Why you called me, right? And why you need to hang up and go get her. Make everything right."

"I'll text her now. Thank you, you're the best."

"I know," she jokes. "Call me later. Let me know how everything went. Make it right."

"Alright, I will. Bye."

I hang up, and separate from the issues with my sister, I miss being home with her. But right now, I need to do what she said and make it right with Clover. The point of all of this wasn't to start a fight, it was to make things better.

That's what I'm going to do.

I look down at my phone.

THE TALE OF MADDY BOEMAN

"What are you talking about?" I asked "She does *what* after school?"

"She volunteers. Swore me to secrecy a while back. She tells her father or brother that she's going on long walks, but the only walk she takes is to the bus station so she can go a town over and volunteer."

I never expected that. Why would she secretly volunteer somewhere and not tell anyone? The whole thing was bizarre. "Where does she volunteer?" I asked.

"The shelter. The one for battered women."

"I know that place," I said. "It's past where Mom used to get us shoes when we were kids—on Union Turnpike, right?"

"Yeah, that's right, Marty's Shoes! I used to love going to that shoe store. Marty had the best lollipops."

"Oh shit, those big round ones! I forgot about those—they were fucking epic. They were worth having to sit there and try on a million pairs of shoes over and over again."

"It's the place on the next corner that used to be abandoned."

"I forgot they made it into a women's shelter. I thought it

was a church or something because of the cross on the outside."

"It's run by the church, but it's not a religious place. They have, like, social workers and psychologists on staff there. It's for women and kids who are running away from abuse."

"How do you know all this?" I asked.

"She took me with her one day. Like I said, she swore me to secrecy, but I think she really wanted someone to know what she was doing."

"Why do you think that has anything to do with where she is right now?" I asked.

"There's a little more to the story than what I told you."

"Hold on." I got up and closed my bedroom door fully so that no one could hear in, and then sat back down and prompted Clover to finish telling me the story. The whole story.

"Do you know Maddy?"

"Maddy?"

"Boeman. Maddy Boeman."

"The 11th grader? The one who's in our math class?"

"Yeah, her."

"Okay. What about her? What's she got to do with this?"

"Apparently Maddy and her mom lived there for four months."

"Oh, shit, really?"

"Uh-huh. This is all coming from Serafina, but I trust that what she told me was true. Maddy and Fina have gym together, and Fina noticed her sitting on the sidelines and never playing. Just sitting, looking sad. So what do you think Fina did?"

"Went over and started talking to her."

"Right. And before you know it she had the girl's life story. Maddy's mom took her and left one night when her dad was working a night shift. Planned it for a month. Made all the arrangements, then waited until the perfect time. She only told Maddy about it the night before. And then, boom, she left everything behind and disappeared."

"What was the father doing?"

"Hitting Maddy's mom. Hitting Maddy sometimes. God knows what else. He was a mean drunk according to Fina, and he told them that he'd kill them both if they ever left him."

"And she did anyway? That took some balls."

"It sure did. It got dramatic. Fina said the dad tried to track them down and they had to have him arrested. He's still in jail now. The school district let Maddy keep coming, but she takes a bus every day."

"To the shelter?"

"No, they left there a while ago. The whole idea is that you only stay until you can get back on your feet. They helped her mom get a job in the area and the school let Maddy keep going even though she technically was living out of the district. Now they live with Maddy's Aunt."

"Jesus. I didn't know any of that. It's crazy, isn't it?"

"What?"

"It's crazy how you can sit two seats away from a person in a class, every single day, for an entire year, and never realize what the hell they're really going through?"

"She could say the same about us, Nate."

"Yeah," I answered. "I guess she could. Parents, huh."

"Parents," she repeated. "But, anyway, Serafina did hours there, and sometimes she'd stay over at Maddy's aunt's house after she did her hours at the shelter."

"It's worth exploring, right? I mean, what harm could come of us taking a bus ride?"

"Tomorrow," she stated. "Today is our birthday, and I

193

want to be selfish for just one day. Let's hang out—do something fun together. Mom and Dad can come, too. Let's just try to be a family for a day without something terrible getting in the way."

It was a strange plea from Clover. She was never sentimental about our family. She always seemed almost embarrassed to be one of us. But on our birthday, I think she just wanted to be celebrated, and there was nothing wrong with that. If anyone deserved a mental break it was Clover.

"You got it. And who knows, maybe Fina will show up tomorrow morning, safe and sound, and this whole thing would have been blown way out of proportion." Clover looks at me, her eyebrow raised up. "Wishful thinking?"

"And then some, Nathan," she said. "And then some."

CONTRADICTORY DNA

.

Clover responds to my third text with a curt 'I'll be back in a second.' While I wait I think about our conversation. Maybe I was too harsh. Just because I wanted to drag all of this family stuff up for a book doesn't mean that she should have to. She's been a good sport. She agreed to spend the day in our old neighborhood, a place we haven't been back to in a very long time. Not only that, but she spent however many hours out of her busy schedule to read my first draft. She could have said no to any of it, but she didn't. She's said yes to everything that I've asked of her without hesitation, that means something.

The part that sucks about this is that I wasn't trying to attack her—I actually meant what I said out of concern, but it came out all wrong. I don't blame her for being pissed, but I need to explain myself. A few minutes after her text I see her walking towards me, a fresh drink in her hand. Leave it to my sister to stop for coffee in the middle of a fight. "Hey." She takes a gulp from her cup and looks at me, waiting to see what I have to say. I don't waste any time with small talk.

"Look, I'm sorry. I didn't mean any of that the way it came out?"

"You mean that I'm a pill popping psycho just like Mom? You sure you didn't mean that?"

"First of all, Mom wasn't a 'pill popping psycho', and neither are you. That isn't what I meant at all. All I meant was that. . ."

"I'm going to turn out just like she did? Be catatonic while my kid runs around the house? Be in therapy into my 60's? Have to abandon my career and become a shell of myself? Which part did you mean?"

I really fucked up. I hit the nerve of all nerves—comparing her to our mom. "None of that. That's not what I was saying. I'm not saying that you were going to become her. But. . ."

"Oh God, here it comes."

"Just listen, will you? Hear me out before you react."

"Fine," she says, visibly upset. "Go ahead."

"Thank you. What I was saying isn't that you're going to be a carbon copy of Mom—but that doesn't mean you're not on a bad path that can lead somewhere similar. Mom was in denial. Mom took too many pills prescribed by too many doctors. She spent her life in a therapist's office and trapped in whatever homes she lived in. I don't want you to be heading down that road, not even realizing that you're on it."

"And you think I'm on it?"

I pause before I step into that land mine of a question. How do I answer her honestly without setting her off again? "Here's what I think. I think that we're the last in a long line of people who have had to overcome a lot to get where we are. What those things are is different for each generation, but the Dunbars—all of us—are made of contradictory DNA. It's like there are two sides of each of us—the white and the black—and they're constantly doing battle."

"You really think that?"

"I do. We all have salvation and destruction right inside of us. Some of us just navigate that contraction better than others. I want you to be one of them." She waits before responding. I know there's a risk in what I'm telling her right now, but unlike last time, it's a calculated one. She needs to hear some of this.

"I'm sorry I freaked out before."

"I'm sorry I upset you. Not what I was going for."

"I like to think I'm different, you know? Maybe it's just wishful thinking. How different can I be with a bathroom cabinet full of anti-depressants?" It's the first time Clover's ever acknowledged having any kind of problem, and it shocks me to hear her say it.

"How long have you been on those?"

"Too long," she says. "I've been having. . . issues since after college. I just pretended that they weren't real. You know when you're getting a cold, but you don't want to admit it because then you'll have to look down the road at days of misery and missing work?"

"Yeah, so you just tell yourself that you have bad allergies to make yourself feel better."

"Exactly. That's what I did with the depression and anxiety. I pretended that they were seasonal allergies—things that would pass soon enough. Things that weren't actually what I should have known they were. It took me years to even speak their names out loud, as if invoking them would make them real. Meanwhile, they were already very real, and by the time I admitted they were haunting me, it was too late. They already had me. All I could do at that point was write stories about it and take way too many pills. So stupid."

It's the most honest confession she's ever made to me, and I listen to every word she's saying, struggling with what to say back to her. Funny how writers can be at a loss for words when it matters the most. "It's not stupid," I assure her. "It's a sign of intelligence that you even know all of this about yourself. And there's no such thing as too late, Clover. If you think you're taking too many pills, then take less of them. I'll help you, whatever you need. If there's one thing we know how to handle in this family it's mental health issues."

"Do we?" she asks.

"We're not Mom and Dad. We're not Angela and Thomas. And we're not whoever the hell came before them that we don't even know about. We're us, and we can get better if we want to."

"Do you. . ." she asks, "ever get any symptoms of anything."

"Did you know about my OCD as a kid?"

"You had OCD?"

"So I guess not. Not *had*—have. I still have it, but I keep it under control. I get a decent amount of anxiety from time to time, and the occasional bout with the big D—but nothing chronic or debilitating like Mom."

"That's good. I'm glad it hasn't grabbed both of us. Maybe that's why I'm so sensitive to all this stuff you're bringing up. I wanted to believe I survived whatever disease this family has—that I dodged Thomas' bullet. But I guess no one gets out alive."

"Some of us do. It's not a kill shot for us, Clover, just a flesh wound. We'll heal. I'll help you."

"Did you really see her Nate?"

"I did. I wish that I could tell you I was hallucinating, or crazy, or just really stressed out, but I really saw her. I saw her life. I saw everything."

"Everything?" she asks.

"I saw it all, Clover," I say, the next words waiting on the edge of my lips. "I saw how she died."

With that declaration, nothing but silence between us.

ALL OF THIS GETS BETTER ONE DAY

I felt like a junior detective as I boarded the bus.

I knew that Clover is going to be pissed because the night before we agreed to go find Serafina together, but when I woke up I knew that it was something I had to do alone. I couldn't tell you why exactly, but something deep inside of me told me to go alone. I didn't bring anything, I just grabbed my bus pass, walked three blocks to the station, and boarded the Q bus up past Union Turnpike to find Serafina.

The ride was short—less than ten minutes, and as we passed Marty's Shoes I felt a tug of nostalgia. I remember how much I hated being dragged there, trying on all those shoes, putting my feet in that wooden thing to make sure it fit. Clover and I complained every minute of those little shopping excursions Mom used to take us on. Now I miss those days.

Once I passed the shoe store my thoughts turned to Fina. What the hell was I doing? I wasn't a cop, or a bounty hunter —I was some asshole riding the Q bus way too early in the morning to find my missing friend. It made no sense. But it was the only thing to do. I asked the driver to stop as soon as we crossed over Union Turnpike, and two blocks later he pulled over. I was the only one who got off at that stop, and I felt like a stranger in a strange land, even though I lived a few minutes away.

After a short walk I saw the shelter. I didn't know if they were open—or if open was a thing for shelters. I had no idea how it worked, but I walked right up to the front door and knocked. I didn't know what to expect, but I heard footsteps approaching. When the doors swung open I felt like I was back in catholic school, as I stood face to face with a priest who looked like he was around my parents' age. He had a gentle expression and pale blue eyes. I didn't know what to say to him, so I stood there silently like an idiot. Luckily, he took pity on me.

"Hello, son."

His voice snapped me out of my stupor, and I remembered how to be a normal person.

"Hi, Father." I stopped there for some reason. I couldn't stop being weird. It was like I expected Fina to answer the door and greet me.

"How can I help you? Are you lost?"

"No, Father," I said. "Actually, I meant to come here. I live over in the Meadows."

"Ah, a local," he joked. "So what brings you here, son. Is everything alright?"

"Actually, no. I'm looking for a friend of mine. I don't know if she's here or not, but I have a feeling that she might be."

"As a resident?" he asked.

"No, Father. I meant as a. . . I guess it would be as a volunteer. Someone told me that Serafina's been working here."

"Serafina?" he asks. "Well, why didn't you say so? Any friend of hers is welcome here."

He opened the doors and let me in—the smile on his face widening the second I said her name. As I went to step through the doorway I heard my name called from behind.

"Well," he said. "There she is now."

"Hi, Nate."

Hearing her voice reminded me that this whole thing was real — that she'd left her house voluntarily for a reason I didn't yet know; that her father had come to our house and interrupted our birthday because he was worried sick; and that, as I stood there, her father was most likely headed to a police station to file a missing person's report on his recently vanished daughter. All that was playing in my head as I turned around to the sound of her voice.

"Hey."

Her eyes met mine, and I remember noticing how unsurprised she seemed to see me—as though my arrival was expected—as though all of this was expected.

"Hey. How did you. . ."

"I was just making friends with Father. . ."

"Barrett," he answered. "Father Barrett. And it's a pleasure to meet you. . ."

"Nathan, but you can call me Nate."

"Nate it is, then. Serafina, we don't need you for a few minutes, so if you want to take some time to talk to your friend here that's fine with me."

"Thank you, Father," Fina answered. She walked past me, through the doors, and took me by the arm. "Is the back room available?"

"Yes," Father Barrett answered. "The Daltons left this morning, the room is free for the time being. You can have whatever privacy you need in there."

I thanked Father again as Fina pulled me towards one of the guest rooms in the back. As she did I looked around. I remember thinking that it didn't look like what I expected it to when Clover described it to me. I guess all the movies I'd seen made me think that it was going to look like a giant homeless shelter—large cots in a big open space with women and kids sleeping on them. But it didn't look anything like that. My examining of the room was short lived, as Fina pulled me into the empty room that Father Barrett motioned her towards, and as soon as our feet were in the door she closed it behind us.

"Are you okay?" I asked. It was a silly question, but the only one that made sense for me to ask.

"Yeah I'm fine, I guess."

"You guess? Where did you sleep last night? Do they know that you. . . that you left home?"

"Sort of. Not really. I told them that my parents know I'm volunteering here until late. They didn't ask too many questions. I don't think they get a lot of volunteers my age because they didn't check anything I told them. Didn't even ask for a phone number where they could reach my dad. And I slept at a friends house."

I knew exactly who that friend was—and now it all made sense. Well, sort of.

"How?" she asked. "How did you find me?"

"Clover. Don't be mad at her, but she told me that you volunteered here so I decided to come. We've all been worried sick."

"Who's we?" she asked.

"Everyone. Me, Clover—my whole family, and more importantly, your whole family. Your dad was at our place yesterday worried sick."

That last part made her snicker. It was a dark kind of sound, and it puzzled me. "What?"

"Nothing," she said. "I wasn't laughing at you. I just. . ."

"What?" I asked again. "What is it? Why did you come here? What aren't you telling me?"

That's when she told me about her dad.

"He used to beat my mom, you know?"

"Who?" I asked.

"Who do you think, Nate?"

"Oh," I said, realizing she was speaking about her father. "I'm sorry, I had no idea, you never. . ."

"You learn not to talk about stuff like that. And I don't mean he hit her one time. I mean he used to beat her. Sometimes right in front of us. You ever notice how scared Damien is of him?"

"Yeah, I have," I answer. "Carmine and I noticed how he was when your dad would call him to check in. I just figured it was 'cause your dad was a little edgy."

"Edgy?" she laughed. "That's one way to put it. Never heard that one before." She laughed again, but not the kind when something's funny, but the kind when you don't know how else to react to something ridiculous you just heard. "The reason Damien's so afraid is because one night, a few years ago, he tried to defend my mom. Dad came home like he did at least a few times a week—reeking of booze and slurring his speech. I guess he didn't like the dinner Mom made that night because he started wailing on her right in the kitchen. Damien had enough, and jumped in between my parents and punched my dad right in the face."

"Damien did this? Our Damien?" It was a terrible story, but I felt a sudden wave of pride at my friend jumping in to defend his mom like that.

"Our Damien." She smiled, like she was proud of her

brother. "He's not like that anymore. Dad beat the hero right out of him that night. Sent him to the hospital. He was there for almost a week."

"Jesus. What the hell did your mom tell them?"

"The usual abused women lies. That time it was that Damien and her had been mugged and attacked on the way home from taking a walk. There was a lot of crime in my old neighborhood, so it wasn't an unbelievable story. That, and the cops were really overworked with homicides and drug cases, so a kid who got his ass kicked wasn't exactly going to get a full investigation going, especially if the mother gave them a story that made sense. And Mom was more than willing to cover for my dad. They fixed Damien up, and he came home a shell of himself—the scared kid you and Carmine play basketball with every afternoon."

"Fina, I don't know what to. . ."

"To say?" she asked, cutting me off. "You mean that you're sorry I'm going through this? That you wished you knew? That a whole lot about me makes more sense now. I've heard all that before, Nate. It doesn't help."

"Heard what before? From who?"

"A year before we moved over by you guys, when Mom got real sick, I told a teacher about everything that was going on. I tried to, at least."

"And he didn't do anything?"

"He was one of those teachers who greeted kids at the classroom door, all corny with his 'good morning students' routine, you know?"

"Like Mr. James?"

"Exactly!" she says, laughing. "Just like Mr. James. He even dressed like him, too. Sports jacket, a book in his hand that I never actually saw him reading. I think it was a prop to encourage us to read more. But, anyhow, this teacher also sometimes touched kids on the shoulder to greet them. He did that to me one morning as I tried to rush past him to my seat. Unfortunately, my dad had grabbed me so hard that he left a mark, so when the teacher squeezed on my shoulder I winced in pain. He looked at me like he knew, or maybe I just wanted him to know what I was going through. Either way he didn't say anything, but I was desperate to tell someone."

Her story sounded familiar. Too familiar. "Is that what happened the other day when I hugged you and you pulled away?" She looked at me and nodded, the embarrassment all over her face. "I knew something was wrong. I flipped out after you left and. . ."

I stopped before telling her the next part. I knew she wasn't with Russell anymore, but I wasn't so sure how she'd react to the news of me beating him up. "What?" she asked. "What did you do?"

"I know that you probably can't control whether you get mad at me or not, but if it's at all possible try not to—I thought I was doing something good."

"You're freaking me out Nate, what did you do?"

"I may have taken Carmine over to Jared's house, called Russell outside, and almost knocked him out. That might have happened."

"What? Jesus, Nate, really?"

"I'm sorry. I didn't know all this about your dad at the time. I knew you were hurt and didn't want to tell me. Russell made the most sense. I wanted to. . ."

"What? What did you think you were doing?"

"I don't even know," I admit. "Told myself after that I had defended your honor, like some medieval knight or something. Or that I was hurting him like I thought he'd hurt you. But looking back I think I just got mad and lost control. Clover tried to stop me. She's always reasonable."

At the mention of my sister's name Fina started crying. I wasn't sure why. "I've been such a bad friend to her. We were so close last year and I've been pushing her away and getting caught up in all my own bullshit. I feel so bad."

"Enough feeling bad, okay? Don't worry about Clover, she's fine and she's a forgiving person. You can talk to her about all that another time. Finish your story about the teacher. So what happened? You told him?"

"Not exactly," she said. "It was English class, and he gave us a writing prompt for homework that we had to bring in the next day. We were supposed to take our greatest fear—whatever that was—and write a short story about it. I wrote about a girl who runs away from home because she's afraid that her father will hurt her if she stays there too much longer."

"And what happened when he read it?"

"He didn't," she answered. "He never saw it."

"How come?"

"Someone else saw it first."

"Oh no, your dad?"

She laughed again. That dark, sad laugh that made me uncomfortable. "My mom, actually. Dad never saw any of my schoolwork. He didn't give two shits about that stuff."

"Your mom threw it away? But why?"

"Because she loved my father. Right up until the end. Can you imagine that? She was in our house, dying, and her only thoughts were to protect that man as much as she could. I'll never forget what she said—she called me into her room and had the paper in her hands. '*You listen to me, Serafina, because I'm not going to be around to teach you all the things that need knowing for much longer. This here—we don't talk about things like this to other people. You father loves you the way he knows how. He loves all of us the only way he knows how, and it's your job now to keep him safe. To know how to keep secrets is part of being a woman, baby, and you'll be the woman of the house when I'm gone.'* Then she tore up my homework right in front of me, and threw the pieces in the garbage pail next to her bed."

If there was ever a moment in my life where I didn't know what to say next, it was that one. I had about twenty different thoughts as I listened to her story, but I understood even then that it was a situation where the right words were required. I just didn't have them yet, so I sat quietly, waiting for her to continue.

"She died a few months later. I got a zero on that assignment, and my dad used part of Mom's life insurance money to move us to The Meadows. You know the rest."

"I'm not sure I do," I said.

"What do you mean?"

"I mean, has this been going on since you've lived here? Is he hurting you? Or Damien? Or both of you?"

"Remember what I told you that night in your room? We're both card carrying members of the Sick Parents Club, Nate, you tell me."

"So why don't you say something? Do something? I don't understand."

"Of course you don't understand. Your parents are good people. I wouldn't expect you to understand."

Your parents are good people. It was a factual statement for her, but for me it was something else, a reminder that having perspective is everything. For all the times I judged my parents and blamed them for all of my problems, I never gave them the credit they deserved for not being people like Mr. Gilmore.

I thought again about what to say—I felt like any words I could string together would be inadequate at worst, clichéd at best. A thousand platitudes ran through my head— *it'll be okay, I'll get you help, don't worry about the future, it'll all work out*. But none of them were the right things to say, and I didn't even believe some of them enough to fake it. So, instead, I only offered. . .

"I'm sorry. For all of it. That all fucking sucks."

"Agreed," she answered. "But hey, what can you do?"

"I'm not sure this is the answer, though. Running away and. . ."

"I didn't run away. I just needed a break. I need breaks sometimes."

"Your dad came over frantic. He's calling the cops. You've been gone for more than twenty-four hours, which means he can file a missing person report on you now, which he probably will. You need to come back before this gets too big to control."

"I'm not going back to that house, Nate." That's when she started to cry, deeply. So deeply that her words were hard to understand. "I don't want to keep secrets anymore. I don't want to be afraid. I don't want to let my house fuck me up more than it already has. Sometimes I don't even recognize myself, Nate. I think weird things, I act out, I hang out around guys like Russell who I shouldn't even give the time of day to. That house is killing me slowly. If I go back there I won't ever leave."

There were no more words after that—just sobbing so deep that it made me cry right along with her. I felt so far out of my league that I didn't know what to do for her except offer my own tears. I don't know how long it went on, it felt like an eternity, but when she finally calmed I wrapped my arm around her and pulled her in close.

"You don't have to go back there, Fina. You don't. But

you do need to tell someone about your dad. It isn't safe for you in that house."

"I should be able to, right? To just dial up the cops or whoever and just tell them my dad's abusive. A teacher, a guidance counsellor, a neighbor, a priest? Only I can't do it. I don't know why. Maybe it's what my mom said to me, or the guilt I know I'll feel doing that to my dad. But I just can't, Nate."

There would be few moments I'd remember with such clarity in my life. Moments where I didn't doubt the effect that time would have on my ability to recall them exactly as they'd happened. She couldn't turn her own father in, but I could. She'd never ask me, and if I'd said the words out loud she would have told me not to do it, so I said something else instead.

"You know, I thought I'd chased you away."

"You?" she asked, furrowing her brow. "How come?"

"I left you something the other day. I think you got it. I thought it might have freaked you out."

The bravery I'd lacked when I dropped my unsigned letter in her mailbox appeared, just like that. I told her without telling her, but as soon as the words left my mouth she realized what I was talking about, and looked at me differently than she ever had before.

"That letter was yours?"

I nodded. "Yeah. I didn't have the balls to sign it."

"I don't know what to say right now."

"You don't have to say anything," I reassured her. "Nothing. I didn't tell you to get a response, I told you so that you'd know the truth. There are bigger things to worry about right now besides my stupid feelings."

"I can't believe that you wrote that," she said. Nothing followed up that thought. Just a little more crying, and her leaning her head gently on my shoulder. I don't know how many minutes passed, but it doesn't matter. I let her lean on me, my shirt getting wet with her tears, as I thought of what to do next.

"You want to know something?" I whispered to her.

"What?"

"I know that all of this gets better one day. I believe that."

"I hope you're right, Nate," she answered softly. "For all of our sakes."

I WOULDN'T CHANGE IT FOR
THE WORLD

The world changed forever. My world. Fina's world. Our world. When I got home Clover was justifiably angry at me, but I stopped the barrage of yelling when I told what happened.

"I knew he was a bad guy!" she yelled. "I fucking knew it!"

Clover wasn't a very good teenager. She didn't curse often, never snuck out of the house or broke curfew, and was generally the complete opposite of your stereotypical teen girl —so when she dropped an F bomb you knew she meant business.

"I never liked him either," I agreed. "But I never thought he would hurt his own kids. I just thought he was kind of a dick. Another sick parent I guess."

"There seem to be a lot of those now, huh?"

"I don't know," I answered. "Maybe there always were. Maybe there always will be. I think every generation thinks they have it worse, but we have it better than anyone." She shot me the are-you-serious look, but I meant what I said. "I'm not saying we don't have problems. We have plenty. But

Mom and Dad never hit us. Never told us we weren't good enough. Never knocked us down. Whatever else you can say, you have to give them that. They try."

"They do try. And you're right, Mom and Dad are good people. They're just. . . damaged."

It was one of those few times that I can remember Clover saying something positive about our family—or at least agreeing with my positive statement. Beggars couldn't be choosers, I took what I could get from her in those moments.

"Speaking of damaged," I said, changing the subject back to our friend. "I feel terrible for Damien and Fina."

"Me too," she said. "So, what are you going to do now that you know?"

"I'm not sure. But I know she won't come back until I do. I think I know."

I knew exactly what needed to be done. Wasn't rocket science. Wasn't brain surgery. I made an anonymous call to the kind of people who needed to know what was going on in the Gilmore household - the rest was up to them.

I told Clover everything about what happened—every detail—every little piece of the puzzle.

Well, sort of.

I didn't tell her what Fina and I said to each other after she told me about her dad, after she asked me for help without really asking me.

She finished crying eventually. It felt like forever. Enough tears to drown in, but not enough to cleanse her home of the sickness that inhabited it. For that she'd need help. But as I was thinking about what to do next, she spoke.

"I loved your letter, you know? Every word. Every sentence."

"You did? I thought it was dumb."

"Dumb? Are you crazy? It's the sweetest thing anyone's ever given me. It's not even close."

All that was to say that she loved my writing, but nothing about what it actually said. I felt bold that day, so, you know, screw it.

"How did it make you feel? The letter?"

To date, the scariest question I've ever asked anyone, ever. I held my breath, waiting for the swift and painful rejection that was sure to come. I didn't care anymore, I just needed to get it out. It was a day for honesty—a day for confessions, and that was the only one I had to offer.

"It made me feel incredible—for as long as I could feel like that. I kept it in my back pocket. It's there right now."

"Well keep it there. If you ever feel lost then I'll write you another. And another after that. Ten letters, if it takes that many, all addressed to Serafina, however many to make you feel better."

She looked at me with red, teary eyes, and smiled. "That sounds like a book title."

"What?"

"Ten Letters to Serafina."

Mr. Gilmore was arrested later that week. An anonymous call to Child Protective Services by a concerned friend who wished to remain nameless.

CPS did what they were required to do—they took Damien and Serafina out of the home for twenty-four hours while they launched an investigation into the allegations against their father. The state of their living conditions alone demanded further action—and it was Damien who gave them all the information they needed for it to become a legal matter. Police came in, Hank was arrested, and the kids were taken out of that hell hole permanently.

Damien and Serafina moved in with their maternal aunt,

who lived about fifteen minutes away from us in a different part of Queens. They both stayed at the school even though their aunt had to drive them each day. We finished the school year. Then the next, then the next. Russell and Jared graduated and moved away—last I heard he was selling jewelry in Manhattan and they'd both gotten caught up in some kind of Ponzi scheme.

So what happened after all that? To my family and me and Fina? Well, dear reader, I have to admit that the Story of Us is a great one, but nonetheless one for another day. A million things between alpha and omega, but it'll have to wait. Another time. Check back later.

For now, don't worry about what happened next, just remember what happened first: a long time ago, my friends and I belonged to a club that no longer exists. We didn't have official meetings, or membership cards. There were no tee shirts, or secret handshakes. Only the bond between us, forged in being raised by the victims of victims, and coming out stronger for it. I used to wish that I came from a different family, that everything about my past had played out differently than it actually did. Now, with the passage of time, I know better. I wouldn't have changed it for the world.

OUR CRAZY CAN BE A GOOD CRAZY

Sometimes the saying of things makes them real. The words can remove them from the recesses of memory or belief, and place them squarely into the living world, like a museum display, for everyone to see. The words I just spoke were the first time anyone's heard what I really experienced that night. It's time to tell the whole story, as best as it can be told.

"I know how that must sound."

"What do you mean you saw how she died?"

"I've never actually said it before, in that way, even in the book." I've been referencing the book all day—but really it isn't a book yet. A book has a cover, it has an editor, it's a fully formed thing. What Clover read, and what I have next to me right now is a draft. There's still time to change things before it becomes a book, and I've been struggling as to how to end the entire thing. This confession is the natural ending, but I've left it out out of embarrassment that people will think that Nathan Dunbar, writer extraordinaire, has lost his mind.

Clover stays quiet. She's always been a skeptic—always demanding enough evidence to fill a courtroom for whatever it was that you were trying to sell her. It's a good quality, but

I have none to offer her right now except my word. I hope that it's enough.

She relents her silence long enough to give me room to explain. "Tell me." She says.

"Do you remember the box? The one that Mom gave us?"

"The magic box? Of course. I remember Dad pulling us into their bedroom before he took us to visit her in the hospital and asking me what I thought it was."

"And do you remember what you said?"

"I remember guessing that it was a magic box, and the surprised face Dad made. What about it, though?"

"I've been thinking about that box a lot lately. It's like that thing held more than just a dollar and a note telling us to get ice cream with Dad. It's like it was a box that held part of our family inside of it, some intangible force that was begging to be let loose."

"Don't you think you're being a little dramatic right now?"

"I'm not speaking literally, don't worry. Just a metaphor. I just think it's telling that Mom gave us something whose very purpose is holding things inside and keeping them secret."

"Why are you telling me this now?" she asks. And when she does I realize that I'm very much in my own head, talking to myself as much as I'm speaking to her.

"Because Angela's story was the ultimate secret our family kept—the taboo we were never to speak of around anyone else in the family, yet it's also the thing that in many ways set us all on the paths we've taken. It's time to open the magic box."

I take a deep breath. I'm out of coffee, but that's probably a good thing. Caffeine would convert energy into anxiety, and the last thing I need while sounding crazy is to look the part. I take another deep breath, my second in as many minutes, and as my lungs fill with air I feel like a runner getting into position, readying my body for an experience I've trained for, but I know will nonetheless be exhausting in its execution. I exhale into the wind, and reach deep into the recesses of my teenaged memory, making sure that the details I'm about to tell my sister—things no one in the world know about—are as accurate as twenty-year-old memories can be.

"The last time I saw her was just like the first time. I mean I saw her, right there, in my room, frozen in time like that picture we have of her in the photo album. You know the one?"

"Yeah, that old black-and-white with her and the family."

"She looked just like she did in that picture. No words again, just that look of calm, her black eyes staring at me, looking into me, practically. She reached out her hand straight in front of her, with a palm up-stretched, as if she waned me to take it, the way you'd do if you were going to lead a person somewhere they were unfamiliar with."

"So what happened?"

When I touched her, I was someplace else—sometime else. It was a police station filled with cops who looked like they were from an old movie. There was a young girl, a teenager but she looked older.

The young girl was pleading with the officer that her father had been acting strange, threatening to push their mother off of the roof. The officer laughed when she said this in her thick Greek accent. "Kid, you know how many times I've told my wife I was gonna push her off the roof if she kept aggravating me? Should I lock myself up?"

The other men who were listening to this frantic girl started laughing hysterically. She wasn't deterred. She just repeated her concern, and assured the officer that she could tell the difference between a joke and a threat, and the longer she spoke the more the officer listened. "If he hasn't done anything then there isn't anything we can do. If you think he's lost his marbles you can have him committed, but your mom would have to sign some papers."

"Do you have the papers?" she asked the officer with a gleam of hope in her eyes. He handed them to her, and she left to run home.

In that instant I was sitting at their table, the girl and her mother, only they couldn't see me. I saw the papers the officer had given the girl spread out on the table in front of a woman with dark hair and pale skin that had was prematurely aged. "Please, Mama, you have to sign these papers. You have to have him committed at the hospital. I swear he's going to do something soon."

The woman dismissed her daughter —moving a finger in a disapproving wave, declaring that she would never lock up her own husband. "He's not okay, Mama, he keeps yelling at a dog that isn't even there. He yells and yells that he's going to beat the dog if he pees on the carpet one more time. I saw him do it. So did Vassily."

Again, the woman dismissed her daughter's concerns. "There's nothing wrong with him, Eleni. He's your father. He's stressed. He works hard for us. He'd never hurt us." The girl got up then, and walked to the room that she shared with her sisters and brothers.

That's when the scene changed again. It was a different time —a few weeks or months from the scene at the kitchen table, but I didn't know how long it had been. For me it was seconds. I was in the room with the kids—all different ages, but some of them looked to be in their early twenties, like the girl, Eleni, and others seemed to be much younger. They all shared a small room, and it was still dark outside from what I could tell.

Suddenly, Eleni got up, as if it were her job to do so. She walked into the living room, then the kitchen, where her mother was preparing food for the family like she probably did every morning. Eleni sat down, and the two of them spoke like mother and daughter.

Then a man appeared. He was fully dressed, as if he was going to work, in a fancy suit with shiny shoes. The man looked very Mediterranean, with a thick black mustache and dark European features. He didn't speak at all. I felt a fear when he came in the room. It felt ominous. It felt like danger, but I didn't know why. And that's when it happened.

Eleni was sitting there, drinking a glass of water. Her

mother's back was to her, as she faced the stove. The man with the black mustache came up behind her, reaching, without hesitation, into his suit jacket pocket, and pulling out a small revolver. He held it to the base of the woman's head, and fired.

The sound. I remember the sound of it. I've never been around guns before, and it wasn't like in the movies, Clover. It wasn't some pop like a firecracker. It was deafening. After the sound and the puff of smoke that followed the woman's body fell, and there was yelling from the kids' bedroom.

That's when my perspective changed. I wasn't watching the whole thing unfold like an invisible person in the house. Everything went sideways, and the point of view shifted upwards in angle. I couldn't move and I could hardly breathe, and I didn't feel any pain, but instead the most incredible sadness I've ever experienced.

I realized then that I wasn't me anymore. I wasn't seeing the rest of the scene unfold through my eyes, I was seeing it through the woman's.

Eleni jumped to her feet, screaming in terror as the man pointed the gun in her direction. It was obvious that he meant to kill everyone, not just his wife. But Eleni wasn't going to be killed that day, not like her mother, not at all. She rushed him as if she already knew this might happen and was prepared for the fact that, one day, she might have to fight her own father to save her life or the lives of her siblings.

By the time the gun was pointed in her direction, Eleni already had both of her hands on her father's gun hand, fighting for control of the small object that had just taken her mother from her. The two of them wrestled for a few seconds before she was able, somehow, to wrestle the gun from his hand. It hit the ground and slid towards my eyes—her eyes— and I heard the noise of metal scraping against floor.

The rest of the siblings came into the kitchen. The screaming was overwhelming. They were all looking at me, yelling and crying. All except the oldest boy, whose name I didn't know. He didn't utter a sound. He just ran towards his father, who by now had grabbed a pair of kitchen sheers, and was trying to plunge them into his own chest repeatedly. The boy grabbed his father and grabbed the sheers, tossing them to the ground, where they found a home not far from the still smoking gun.

The boy and Eleni wrestled the man with the black mustache to the ground, as the neighbors started to pound on their front door. Then I heard Angela's thoughts as if they were my own.

"Not my babies," she said. "Don't hurt my babies."

Soon the scene I had just witnessed went away. All the sounds disappeared, slowly, until there was nothing but the ever-fading kitchen, creeping out of focus. The sadness encompassed me so completely that it felt like a heavy blanket being placed over my body, and as the images disappeared, the darkness came. It came slowly at first, like a promise to end the suffering, and then it sped up so quickly that I couldn't perceive it's happening, like falling asleep.

And then. . .

"What?" Clover asks. "And then what happened?"

"I woke up."

"And???"

"And nothing. I woke up, or whatever you want to call it. I came back to now; well, now back then I mean. It just ended, and I was sitting in my room again, like always."

"And what did Angela say? What did she do?"

"Nothing. She was gone. I never saw her again after that night. Maybe I never even saw her then."

What happens next I'm not ready for.

"Yes, you did, Nathan," she said, and she did it with such conviction that I looked at her, stunned. The years of disbelief and judgement falling by the wayside in an instant. "You saw her, and as crazy as I'm about to sound, I think that she saw you too."

"What do you mean she saw me?" I was confused. I didn't know what she meant, but I could hear the sincerity in her voice.

"What I mean is that maybe, just maybe, you have this whole thing backwards. Or confused, at the least. Just consider it. Maybe, it wasn't just about you learning the story of her past, it was about her wanting to see into the future that was denied to her. To see the relatives she'd never meet, to make sure that you weren't a man like all the other men. Maybe that's why she chose you and not me, or Mom or Dad. Now who sounds nuts, huh?"

Her words were profound, but more than that they were surprising to me. In all the years that followed my three visitations I'd never even considered to look at it from the point of view she was describing. I always assumed that Angela appeared to teach me something; to explain to me why things were the way they were in my home; why I had parents who were so damaged that they may never have been right again. I thought she was there to explain my trauma to me, but maybe, if Clover was right, that Angela wasn't only there to teach, but also to learn.

"Uhh!" I yelled so loud that the pigeons flew away and the squirrels scurried away from their spots on the trees.

"What is it?"

"I wish. . . I wish we'd talked about this years ago, Clov. I really do."

"Hey, better late than never, right?"

"Better late than never. So I guess you don't still think I'm crazy?"

"Of course I do. We're all crazy, Nathan. Crazy is our family crest, for God's sake. But who's to say that's a bad thing. We're not like the others before us. Our crazy can be a good crazy, if that's not an oxymoron."

"It's only an oxymoron if we let it be. Let's reclaim the narrative here, huh?"

"It's a deal."

◇◇◇

As the sun sets over the Oak Grove I look around one last time, trying to take the sights and smells into my adult memory. Already the childhood ones are starting to fade, and one day they'll be barely perceptible fragments lost to wherever discarded memories find themselves.

I offer Clover a moment of unfettered editorial power. "Is there anything you think I should change? Or anything you want me to take out?" She looks me straight in the eye, the surprise on her face so obvious that it's near impossible to hide it. She waits a second, thinking about my unexpected question, and then gives me a hug. "What was that for?" I ask, my turn to be surprised.

"Don't change a single thing, you hear me? Not one detail. Not a single thing about what you remember. I'll be mad at you if you do."

Every now and then my sister really surprises me. "You sure?"

"Never been more sure of anything. This book is your truth, and I'd never tell you to remove or change anything in it. Get it to your editor, get a cover, and get it to print."

"Yes, Ma'am," I joke. Even though some of the memories inside aren't happy, I feel nothing but happiness and gratitude that my sister accepts what I've written. She's the only real family that I have left.

"Just one question," she continues.

"Yeah."

"How are you finishing it?"

"What do you mean finish?" I ask. "It's finished."

"No it isn't," she says. "I think you need to add something. A real ending."

"Well I still have to finish that other thing for *The New Yorker*..."

"I know," she interrupts. "Do that. Chronicle the crime as

best you can. But this is something different. This is the story of our family, and it needs to be finished."

"How do you mean?" I ask, confused.

"I think that you need to put something in about what happened after all that. With Mom, with everything. Finish the story."

With Mom. I hear the rest of her words, but it's those two that linger in my mind. Ideas never come when you want them to. They come at the most unexpected moments, when you least expect them. And, as in right now, they sometimes come from the strangest of sources.

"I'll finish the story, I promise."

"So what's the next one going to be about?" she asks me. It's a good question, but I'm not even thinking about that right now.

"Who knows," I answer. "One thing at a time."

"You know we're always thinking about the next one."

"True," I tell her. "And any other time I'd have an answer for you. But this might be the first time I've never even thought about my next book while writing my current one." I look down at my watch and my eyes widen. "Oh, shit, I've gotta get going, my wife's gonna kill me if I'm too late."

"Has she read this yet? Does she even know you wrote it."

"Every word," I answer. "I have to give her credit, the book was actually her idea. I'd be insulted if she didn't read it. It's practically about her."

"True. Tell her I say hi, okay? Tell her I don't care how pregnant she is, she needs to get on the phone and call me. I miss our talks."

"I will. Hopefully she wasn't that sick today."

"Isn't she past all that?"

"It's a myth—the morning sickness thing. It's just sickness."

"Poor thing. She by herself while you and I sat around all day?"

"Her brother was over in the morning. I'm not sure if he's still there. I'll be home soon enough. Did I tell you we're doing one of those stupid gender reveal parties? Not my idea, but you have to come."

She slaps herself on the forehead. "Holy shit, Nathan, I forgot. You found out, didn't you?"

"We did. But instead of just telling people I have to go get a special cake made and. . . I'm not even sure what else, there's a whole ritual. She showed me the websites."

Clover laughs. "Can I know? Or do I have to wait to see the color of the cake like everyone else?"

"It's a girl. Her name is going to be Laylah."

"Laylah? That's beautiful Nathan. I love it. And thanks for telling me, you know I hate waiting."

"I know you do. And you don't have to thank me, we're family. If anyone should know, you should. Love you."

"You too," she says, grabbing onto me for one last twin hug. "And seriously, tell Serafina to call me, okay?"

"I will."

The drive home is only a few hours, but along the way I'll have plenty of time to do what I love the most—think. But my thoughts aren't filled with memories of Mom's depression, or the ghost of Angela. For the first time in a while all of my thoughts are to the future, to the stories that need to be told, and to the baby growing inside of my wife.

I can't wait to be home.

ONE MORE STORY

I forgot to tell you this one, but better late than never, right? Well I learned something from the writing of this book—about memory, about family, about how to see the past with a different set of eyes. When I think of Mom now, I don't just think about crying, or anxiety, or despair. Those things are there, to be sure, and they always will be because they're part of her story. But there's one memory in particular that always comes back to me when someone asks me about who my mom was.

I think about that time she came to my school to pick me up.

I'm getting ahead of myself. You remember when I said I had to leave school for most of my 7th grade year because I assaulted that kid Eric? Well my parents couldn't home school me—Dad worked days and Mom was trying to go back to school again, so that left only one option—catholic school.

Now understand that untold volumes remain to be written on that score—*The Adventures of Nathan*—*come see him as he takes on the evil controlling priests masquerading as teachers!* Tales for another day. For right now understand this —however I stood out in public school, catholic school was amplified to a ten. The atheist free thinker wasn't welcomed in those parts, yet those parts were all that remained due to my losing control that day in the cafeteria.

There was one boy in particular—Ryan—who went out of his way to shit on me. He wasn't your standard bully. There were no physical threats, or throw downs on the playground while the sisters tried to keep watch over us. His bullying was psychological. He'd pretend to be my friend only to later tell me he wanted no part of me. He'd tell other kids rumors about me so they'd cut me off. He isolated me, and got pleasure out of doing it. This went on for some time. My dad —being simple in his worldview—told me to fight the kid. Hit him, then he'll never mess with you again.

No! my mom shouted. That's what got him there in the first place. Violence isn't the answer, Nathan—two wrongs don't make a right. That was her expression. I heard it at least quarterly—more if I did an usually high amount of dumb shit.

For once, I preferred Dad's solution, but I knew it wasn't something I could actually do, which was a shame because I could have fucked Ryan up with one hand tied up. But that solution was closed to me. I left that conversation dejected, anticipating another few months of shit.

Then it happened.

Dismissal came, as it always did, after a long day of bullshit. I was drained—my mind a mix of excitement to be out of that place, and a stupefied pile of mush from all the unnecessary facts I had to learn. 2:45 signaled the final bell, where we ended the day lining up at the doors that led to the outside steps. They finally opened, signifying the daily parole from the educational prison where I was forced to pray before every class.

That's when I saw Mom. Nothing unusual in that, she picked me up every day because the school was fifteen minutes away from where we lived. No matter how she was feeling at that time, she was there for me every day. Only that day she didn't look frail or tired, as she sometimes did. She looked angry—like she was standing with a purpose other than taking me home. I found out what that purpose was.

It was a little tradition that when I made it down the steps Mom would take my bag. I don't know why she did that, but she did, every single day. I was old enough to carry my own stuff, and that summer I'd finally grown a little taller than her, but she was still my mom, and maybe it was her way of reminding me of that. Anyways, that day she didn't take my bag, barely acknowledged me. Once I stood next to her I waited for her to move, but she didn't. Just a Mom statue, watching the doors with all the focus of an owl studying the movements of a field mouse.

That's when Ryan came out, the dumb, cocky smile he always wore on full display for the neighborhood to see. As he walked down the stairs Mom watched and waited, and that's when I knew how Mom planned on making this all better for me.

When Ryan walked past, Mom followed. She scruffed the kid, like a Mama lion, grabbing him by his starched uniform collar and dragging him over to the side yard adjacent to the playground. To this very day I don't know what was said, but Ryan nearly shit himself right there on the spot, and he never bothered me again after that day.

Maybe that was the wrong thing to do. I don't know. I'm not here to stand in judgment. It was a different time and she was a different kind of parent.

But that day taught me something that I didn't realize until years later, when I looked back on Mom defending me despite any consequences. It taught me that maybe, just maybe, being in the Sick Parents Club wasn't something to be embarrassed by, or ashamed of. Maybe, despite the ridicule, and the pointing, and accusations of how weak it made me, it was an honor all along— the first chapter in my very own origin story.

EPILOGUE

I've come a decision. It wasn't easy, and it wasn't without a lot of self-reflection, but I know that it's the right thing to do.

The Sick Parents Club is no longer accepting applications. We're closed. Done. Caput. We had a good run, but I'm turning in my membership card.

We don't need the club anymore, because we can't let who we were, or who we come from, define who we're going to be. That part is a choice, and I choose to just be Nathan. Clover is a successful writer who's working hard to overcome her issues; Serafina is a teacher, finally putting her need to help people to good use, for kids who are way worse off than any of us ever were. Carmine became a successful chef, and now he has his own food cart, a beautiful wife, and two great sons. We see them a few times a year. Damien got a job working as a roadie for WWE—his dream job—now he gets to watch all the wrestling he wants from the best seats in the house.

As for me, I'm just happy.

The writing of this book has been transformative. It hasn't changed who I am, but it has changed my relationship to my past. I've spent decades of my life trying to understand why I saw what I did, and analyzing what was real and what wasn't, and how all of those things were connected to one another, if they were at all. The jury's still out I suppose. I'll let you decide for yourself. But in my maturity, I've come to realize that it doesn't really matter.

It happened, whether it happened or not.

Instead of torturing myself over it, I've recently started asking myself what lessons can be learned from all that I know about the women in my family? Instead of focusing on the bad of their lives—the evils visited upon them, and the harm they sometimes did to others, I instead ask myself what good can come of all I've experienced? Maybe this book is the answer. Like Mom said, I've tried to say that thing with which I labor. I've tried to tell our story from my unencumbered imagination. In that, I hope I've done her proud.

But I've been struggling with how to end the story. The beginnings are the easy part—it's seeing the stories through to the finish line that separates the real writers from the fake. As I sat at home the night I got back from Queens, my pregnant wife slept next to me, and as I stared at her belly I understood how to end it all—I understood how to close the Sick Parents Club forever.

Soon I'll be the father of a baby girl—a little thing whose life I'll be tasked to protect and guard. I wonder, what will she make of all of this once she knows? How will I tell her about the women in her family? How can I let her know that she's a link in an unbroken chain that predates all of our collective memories? That's when the answer comes to me. I get out of bed and sit on the floor. My laptop is next to the bed, and I open it on the floor so as not to wake Serafina. My fingers start their tapping again, only this time the sensation is more than perceptible.

I don't even know your name yet.

Right now, you're just a bump sticking out from the special shirts your mom had to buy to accommodate how big you're growing inside of her. It makes me think of how scary a thing it must be to be born—the cold sensations hitting your newborn skin for the first time; a bunch of strangers putting their hands all over you; the artificial lights shining so brightly in new pupils.

Being born is an act of bravery, and I know that you're going to do it bravely. You get that from your grandmother. I wanted to tell you all about her, if you'll indulge your dad for a few words. From shaky three-year-old legs, I used to look up at her like ancient Man must have looked up to the Sun; wonder in my eyes, amazement, awe. Why? Because even when I was so small that the top of my head barely reached her knee, even then I felt it; I knew her strength, and even then, I knew it would always keep me safe from the dangers of this world.

I come from the strongest of women, and strong women make iron-born babies. Your grandma was just one in a long line—the strongest of them all—but there were many others. Your mom is one also, and so too will you be. You come from the women whose iron was forged in the fires of history—in the violent struggle to survive when it made no sense to do so. They were the type of women who put their fragility on the back burner and found ways to just make life happen—all of them—the collective her that comprise your lineage.

There are inadequate words I could use: brave, self-sacrificing. If you ascribed her such traits she'd reject them outright—no thanks—no compliments, no accolades, no awards necessary. When I remember your grandma, long after Cancer robbed you of the right to sit on her lap and hear her voice, I remember her strength first.

Iron.

You'll understand one day, I promise, but for now just take Daddy at his word. Remember that fortitude is inherited. It lives in the genes, in the heart, in the eyes that look upon this world.

You have her strength because I do—I'm passing it to you as it was passed to me long ago. It was born of pain that you need never experience to have its benefits; born of a life I can only tell you about, and I will. But that strength is yours now, and no one can ever take it from you, even though many will try.

Oh the stories I can tell you one day! Like that one time those kids were picking on me at school. She marched down there when school let out, grabbed that kid who was messing with me by the scruff of the neck, like a mama lion, and dragged him aside. She told him what I always want you to remember: when you mess with a mother's family you mess with her as well. It was a small miracle your grandma didn't get arrested that day. She could have spent the night in jail instead of cooking me dinner and putting me to bed. But that kid never bothered me again

Iron. Forged in surviving; in living, when living made no sense.

When you get bigger you'll learn all about great women in history—queens, suffragettes, feminist leaders. That's all good. That's all fine. But you have your own history to learn first—those women who didn't make the pages of the books they'll pass out to you in school. Never forget this—your women are no less great for the omission of their stories from those books. You may remember their names or you may not.

You'll see only a few of their faces, mostly in pictures that will look so very old to your eyes.

But all you have to do is remember what's important: that their history is your inheritance—the greatest gift you can be given. And know that you, too, will be one of those great women; and that one day, from shaky little legs, your babies will look up at you as though you were the Sun.

AFTERWORD

"Before we leave the ghosts to argue over it"
By Alexandra Santiago DiBiaso

There's beauty in choosing to willfully live, despite every
reason it should not be so. Too many times people in my
family had to make that choice—too many times I've seen
what that choice can cost. I remember the weight of it, in
their eyes, and in others I've seen since. It's humbling. It also
makes much of the frivolity of life excruciating. My grandma
was never frivolous—she had no use for it. The closest she
got was when she took me to Graceland when I was twelve. I
saw her eyes light up on that trip in a way I didn't know they
could. She was in her late sixties, and I always wondered if
that light had been there all along.

But I'm thankful to be able to bear witness to this story,
and to the tragedy that struck my family so long ago.

It's not lost on me that it is the last member of my
generation that's chosen to try and account for this tale. He's
the last to know it this way. He is the last to have seen the

wreckage first hand, so it is rightfully his experience with it to share before we leave the ghosts to argue over it.

From where I now sit I have the distance afforded me by the will and grace of my loved ones—those who faced down that bullet and all the ricocheting it did through my family over the last eighty years. The existence of my point of view is why I know that the destruction that created this Club is now over. Now the story can be told. I know the damage that was done from that bullet and I know that I, and my cousin, have paid all we needed to in order to ensure that our babies will know this as they know many tragic stories—from the outside.

The women you meet in this tale are righteous warriors, and sometime perpetrators, and all victims and victims of victims to one degree or another. They came to their way of living without choice. Survival doesn't allow for it. So it is ironic that the protection they needed, they wanted, and that they sometimes attempted to give, also served as its own weapon. Being isolated from those you love, even if that isolation is meant to protect, does it's own kind of damage. That's the problem with generational violence—you don't have to be there to get hurt.

For better or worse, I'm glad I learned the many things my grandma demanded of me. Her life taught me that choice is itself a luxury, like the fine clothes and beautiful things that she bought and bestowed upon me; like that which she herself craved most, but was never afforded—an education.

For Grandma, education was the key to a way of life always out of reach for her. So, for her, my own college degree was intimately tied into the American dream that brought her through Ellis Island at age eleven. Sadly, I couldn't understand that entirely until I had a daughter, ten years after my grandma was gone.

I count my blessings of distance and time and birthright. My grandmother wore blinders, my Aunt wore armor and my great Aunt served as the mother she never was allowed to be. With them all I could do no wrong, they filled me with the strength pride and confidence they were denied.

Their legends carry them on to immortality.

For my grandma, especially, like my father before me, she felt I was the blessing from the gods—the suffering made right. Unlike her daughter and sisters, I was spared the horrors of her past. In my direction, the bullet slowed.

Now, all these years later, I feel obligated to bear witness, to forgive more and judge less, to say what I saw, in all of its beauty and horror—to love them all through the truth, but at an arms length, when necessary. Judging the decisions and arguing with ghosts is a task I have learned to leave for others, but I mourn the lives they all could have had.

I protect not for me, but for those who come next. So, in that way, I'm no different than the women who came before me. I've learned everything I need to do—and not to do—for those girls who come after me.

We were lucky to have had the women in my family, and we were luckier still for the women who protected us from them. So to all those who suffered the wrong doing of others, to all those who hurt because they hurt, and to those who either jumped in front of the bullet or were thrown in its path, it's over.

The Club is no longer accepting new members.

ACKNOWLEDGMENTS

To Jessica Hildreth, for making what might be my favorite cover, ever.

To my ARC team, for taking the time and effort to read this book and help make it a success (in no particular order): Michaela Zankl, Lisa Hemming, Sandra Foy, Heather Swan, Shirley Werner, Mandy Demaree, Danielle Brass, Monica Cottrell Randau, Stephany Snell, Laura Albert, Carol Scheufler, Lg Reads, Angelique Burns, Katrina Haynes, Karen Tartaglia, Joann Stearns, AnnaMarie Hay, Debbie Eichler, Cathy Lane-Zaffuto, Maria Rivera, Shelly Reynolds, Ann Zimmer, Melanie Stevenson, Amanda O'Brien, Stephanie Mcknight-Bailey, Sue Ouellet, Teresa Guthrie Lara, Clare Fuentes, Tammy Lynn, Tina Laurelli, Sandra Cohen, Teri Ditchman, Amanda Lee, Megan Asmus, Catherine Ingalls Hussein, Jessica Laws, Kara J Coens, Erica Kowalski, Consuelo Marron, Monica L. Murphy, Cheryl Johnson, Mary Dikeman Probst, Sara Gross, Wendy De Jesus, Gwendolyn Kohn, Maria Esther Jiron, Amanda Kristine Mann, Sandi Sierra, Bookluvin Rose, Connie Snyder, Janeen Phillips, Chelle Underwood, Amy Horton,

Kitka Buchanan, Nicole Stegmeier, Heather Rollins Himmelspach, Ches Daniele, Sarah Allen, Geri Lambre Nelson, Angelina Smith, Rebecca Kleckner, Carol Scheufler, Katrina Mari Swift, Jennifer Willison, Jill Bourne, Jennifer Rusher Minton, Susan Montejo, Jennifer Marie, Tammy Lynn, Kathleen McGinn Jarrach, Katryna McClung, Bonnie Bracken, Brandy Freeman, Crystal Waldele PA, Carolyn Nunley, Cindy Hughes, Stephany Snell, April Mansfield, and Sandra Cohen.

To my readers, for their continued support on my passion projects.

And a special thank you to my cousin, Alex, for contributing her words and making the book complete. It wouldn't have been the same without you! Love you.

NEWSLETTER SIGN UP

Dear Readers,

Thank you so much for all of your amazing support! Please sign up for my NEWSLETTER so that we can stay in touch, and you can have access to all my giveaways, new releases, and cover reveals. Don't worry! You'll never be spammed, shared, or sold, and I only send a few emails a year.)